KIDS IN MOTION™

A Creative Movement and Song Book

Created and Written by
Julie Weissman

With Music Produced by
Greg Scelsa and Steve Millang
for Youngheart Records

Edited by Ronny S. Schiff
Cover Designed by David Haight*
Photographs by Wynn Miller
Educational Consultant Carolyn Mosoff
*Logo concept based on the original design by Esther Kwan

KIM Productions / Little House Music / Gregorian Chance Music
Treasury of Tunes / Gallery of Songs
Divisions of Youngheart Records

HL® Hal Leonard Publishing Corporation
7777 West Bluemound Road P.O. Box 13819 Milwaukee, WI 53213

Acknowledgments

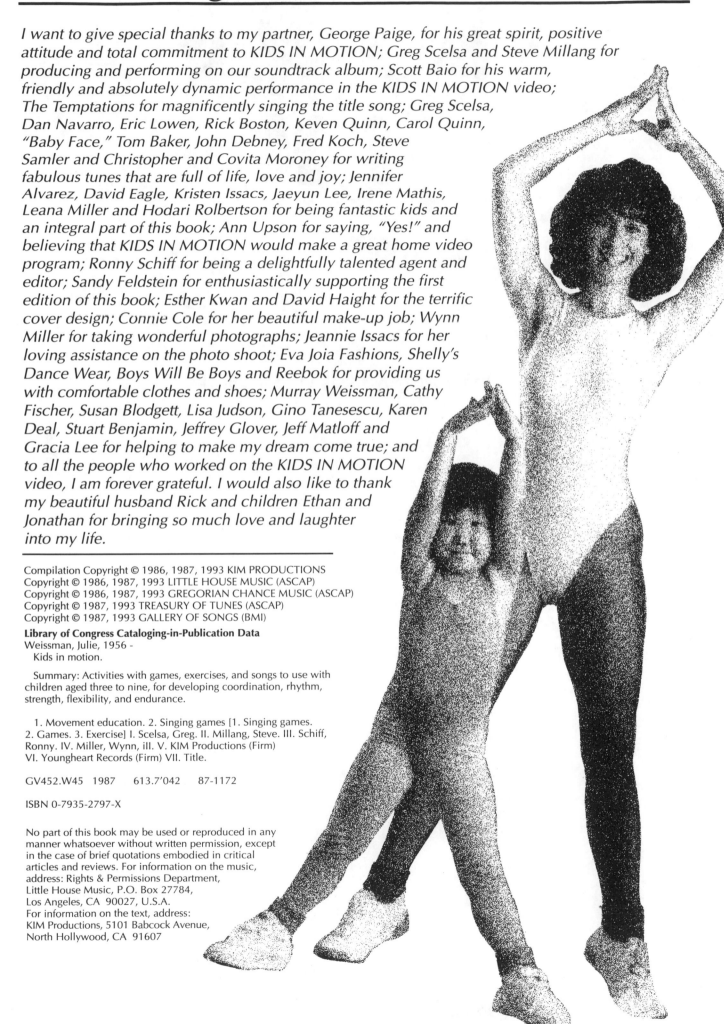

I want to give special thanks to my partner, George Paige, for his great spirit, positive attitude and total commitment to KIDS IN MOTION; Greg Scelsa and Steve Millang for producing and performing on our soundtrack album; Scott Baio for his warm, friendly and absolutely dynamic performance in the KIDS IN MOTION video; The Temptations for magnificently singing the title song; Greg Scelsa, Dan Navarro, Eric Lowen, Rick Boston, Keven Quinn, Carol Quinn, "Baby Face," Tom Baker, John Debney, Fred Koch, Steve Samler and Christopher and Covita Moroney for writing fabulous tunes that are full of life, love and joy; Jennifer Alvarez, David Eagle, Kristen Issacs, Jaeyun Lee, Irene Mathis, Leana Miller and Hodari Rolbertson for being fantastic kids and an integral part of this book; Ann Upson for saying, "Yes!" and believing that KIDS IN MOTION would make a great home video program; Ronny Schiff for being a delightfully talented agent and editor; Sandy Feldstein for enthusiastically supporting the first edition of this book; Esther Kwan and David Haight for the terrific cover design; Connie Cole for her beautiful make-up job; Wynn Miller for taking wonderful photographs; Jeannie Issacs for her loving assistance on the photo shoot; Eva Joia Fashions, Shelly's Dance Wear, Boys Will Be Boys and Reebok for providing us with comfortable clothes and shoes; Murray Weissman, Cathy Fischer, Susan Blodgett, Lisa Judson, Gino Tanesescu, Karen Deal, Stuart Benjamin, Jeffrey Glover, Jeff Matloff and Gracia Lee for helping to make my dream come true; and to all the people who worked on the KIDS IN MOTION video, I am forever grateful. I would also like to thank my beautiful husband Rick and children Ethan and Jonathan for bringing so much love and laughter into my life.

Library of Congress Cataloging-in-Publication Data
Weissman, Julie, 1956 -
  Kids in motion.

  Summary: Activities with games, exercises, and songs to use with children aged three to nine, for developing coordination, rhythm, strength, flexibility, and endurance.

  1. Movement education. 2. Singing games [1. Singing games. 2. Games. 3. Exercise] I. Scelsa, Greg. II. Millang, Steve. III. Schiff, Ronny. IV. Miller, Wynn, ill. V. KIM Productions (Firm) VI. Youngheart Records (Firm) VII. Title.

GV452.W45 1987   613.7'042   87-1172

ISBN 0-7935-2797-X

Contents

Foreword

This book is one of the greatest gifts any parent or teacher can offer a child. Julie Weissman provides a brilliant, step-by-step approach through a wide variety of movement and dance activities, offering a unique combination of body movement, exercise, and music.

"Kids In Motion: A Creative Movement and Song book" focuses on children's feelings, thoughts, creativity, and imagination, as well as their physical well-being. All of the activities in this book have a special purpose, without ever losing sight of the fact that kids just want to have fun!

Working on the "Kids In Motion" video was a great experience for me and I discovered, first hand, how responsive kids are to Julie's concepts. She's made it very easy for parents and teachers to share her creative movement ideas with children over and over again.

Many years of experience, research, and hard work have gone into the production of "Kids In Motion," and I know you and your children will benefit enormously from it.

HAVE FUN!   Sincerely,

Introduction for Parents and Teachers

KIDS IN MOTION is a creative movement program especially designed for boys and girls, ages three to nine. It is a comprehensive program of physical fitness that fosters young children's total development. Through a series of movement games, exercises and songs, children develop mind/body coordination, a sense of rhythm, strength, flexibility and endurance. Body awareness is increased as children become more familiar with each individual body part and the infinite ways of moving. Children develop self-esteem as they learn and master a wide variety of physical skills.

KIDS IN MOTION provides experiences that encourage children to appreciate the similarities and differences among their peers. They learn to respect themselves and others. Perception and comprehension are greatly increased when children are given the opportunity to physically interpret what they are learning. Reading, listening and language skills are sharpened through the total participation that this special program provides. KIDS IN MOTION develops creative expression and inspires children to incorporate imagination into every aspect of their lives.

How to Use this Book

KIDS IN MOTION is divided into two parts and the activities in each of the twelve chapters have easy-to-follow instructions, many with music and corresponding photographs. The instructions are written in simple, direct language that children easily understand. At the heading of every chapter, the purpose behind each group of activities is outlined and there is a glossary that defines important movement-oriented words. The twelve chapters in the book follow the same format as the KIDS IN MOTION video and offer additional activities as well.

When planning a KIDS IN MOTION session, you can choose any of the activities in the book. However, it is a good idea to start with some of the warm-up exercises from *BODY ROCK* or *BODY TALK* before proceeding with other activities. Also, make sure everyone is wearing comfortable shoes and clothing and that you will be moving on a soft surface.

At the conclusion of every chapter is a song and a lesson plan. Each song incorporates the activities from the beginning of each chapter. When you want to share a specific song with your children, follow the directions in the lesson plan, or practice the words and movements in single lines first. Encourage children to sing-along and then sing and dance the entire song together. Each lesson plan includes information on how to reinforce positive behavior and how to handle possible problems specifically related to the activities in every chapter. There are also two songs that are specially geared for the important quiet time activities.

Following each activity are the measure numbers that correspond to the measures in the music incorporating the specific activity. (All of these songs can be found on the KIDS IN MOTION soundtrack Lp or cassette.)

Percussion instruments, such as drums, rattles, cymbals, wrist bells and tambourines, can be used by the leader during a movement session. These instruments are inexpensive and available at music stores.

Finale

KIDS IN MOTION is enjoyable for children to do together. The program gives you, the parent or teacher, an opportunity to spend quality time with your children and introduces new ideas for creative indoor and outdoor activities. Most importantly, KIDS IN MOTION teaches children that learning is a lot of fun!

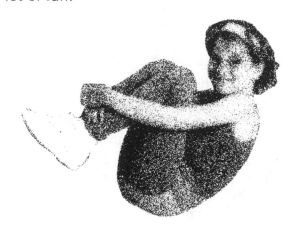

Julie Weissman

While working as a pre-school teacher, Julie Weissman, whose degree is in child development and dance, decided to offer a creative movement class to her students. It was a huge success, and Julie soon became the dance specialist for several schools and began presenting private creative movement classes in schools, health clubs and studios throughout Los Angeles. Julie created a thriving enterprise and called it, KIDS IN MOTION.

While conducting KIDS IN MOTION classes, Julie discovered the importance of incorporating movement concepts that are relevant to children. She noticed that children's concentration and participation were greater when there was a sense of purpose attached to what they were learning. So, Julie and her students began dancing about many things: They danced about feelings, nature, animals and food. They spelled words and did mathematical equations with their bodies. They danced and acted out poems and fairytales. KIDS IN MOTION became a complete program of physical fitness, combining children's natural love of and joy in movement and music with concepts they were learning at home and school.

After offering her program throughout Southern California for several years, Julie realized that KIDS IN MOTION could be structured into a home video program. The idea of providing children with an educational program that encouraged them to participate with the activities on the television screen, excited Julie tremendously. She read and researched extensively on children's passive viewing habits, their junk food consumption and the large number of children that were in poor physical shape. That was enough to make Julie completely devoted to getting KIDS IN MOTION into production for home video. And that she did. Together with producer George Paige, she co-produced and performed in KIDS IN MOTION, starring actor Scott Baio and seventeen children for CBS/FOX VIDEO.

Julie then thoroughly investigated the children's music field, eventually joining with Greg Scelsa and Steve Millang of Youngheart Records. She found the Youngheart philosophy—encouraging children to feel good about themselves in a non-competitive, non-threatening environment—to be compatible with her own, and their delightful, contemporary movement-oriented music to be the perfect sound for KIDS IN MOTION.

Greg and Steve produced the soundtrack album consisting of fourteen original songs, several of which Greg wrote and all of them incorporating the KIDS IN MOTION concepts. The other songs were written by Dan Navarro, Eric Lowen, Rick Boston, Kevin Quinn, Carol Quinn, "Baby Face," Tom Baker, John Debney, Fred Koch, Steve Samler and Christopher and Covita Moroney.

Shortly after the video and album were in production, Julie started to write this KIDS IN MOTION book. She decided that the segments on the video would be the chapters in the book, with each chapter offering many more activities and the music for each song.

Julie's primary focus is to provide young children with learning experiences that encourage them to feel good about themselves and the world around them. She feels that if children have a base of self-respect, confidence and knowledge they will discover, imagine and create.

Youngheart's Greg & Steve

The music of Greg Scelsa and Steve Millang of Youngheart Records is joyful, educational, enriching and just plain fun! It helps children learn basic skills, encourages creative play, promotes the understanding of personal relationships, shows them how to relax, and how to discover the world around them.

Known to their fans simply as "Greg & Steve," Greg Scelsa and Steve Millang have become top stars in children's educational music in an extraordinary way: they combined their talents with good business sense. They not only write and perform their own material, but because of their true concern for children and a desire never to compromise any facet of production, they also recorded, produced, marketed, designed and sold their own recordings and leader's guides right from the start.

These energetic and animated performers began developing their material during the time they were teacher's aides in Los Angeles area schools. Working individually, they both found that adding music to instruction was a wonderful teaching tool. They joined forces, sharing ideas and philosophies.

By 1975, Greg and Steve had so many requests to put their games and songs on tape that they decided to assemble everything and make a record. Little by little, the first WE ALL LIVE TOGETHER recording and leader's guide were completed and the record company established.

As Youngheart grew, they added more recordings to the WE ALL LIVE TOGETHER series, increasing the range of imaginative activities and learning experiences with their upbeat music and cohesive philosophy.

To add more musical dimensions, they then produced ON THE MOVE with its vibrant rhythms for creative play and exercise; QUIET MOMENTS with its restful themes to give children a chance to discover the pleasure of relaxation and reflection; and the

entertaining, KIDDING AROUND, which helps children learn new motor skills, sing along, develop better language skills, and most of all, have fun!

Greg and Steve are so popular now that they spend a great deal of time criss-crossing the U.S.A. and Canada appearing in concerts for children and families and conducting workshops for teachers. They have been guests on numerous radio and television shows, as well as headliners for many educational conventions. In fact, these conventions, such as the National Association for the Education of Young Children, National Headstart Association, and the Music Educators National Conference, play a major role in their travels.

When Greg and Steve were approached by Julie Weissman to produce and write some of the music for her KIDS IN MOTION video, Greg said, "We fell in love with the concept, with Julie's wonderful activities combining music and movement. . . so compatible with our own concepts."

"Watching Julie in action with the children was so joyful. Plus her enthusiasm and energy for the KIDS IN MOTION project was boundless! Working together with Julie, the production staff and the children on the video, as well as on the recordings and on this book, has been a gratifying and growing experience!"

It all goes together with the Youngheart philosophy which encourages children to feel good about themselves in a non-competitive, nonthreatening environment. Working together. . . playing together. . . living together.

Kids In Motion

The Body Rock *Easy Warm-Ups*

The Purpose:

THE BODY ROCK helps children develop coordination, body awareness and a movement vocabulary as they learn to warm-up each part of their body. This aerobic activity encourages children to use their imaginations as they strengthen their muscles and build endurance.

Kids' Glossary

Rock 'n' Roll = A type of popular music with a strong, rhythmic beat that is usually played on amplified instruments, and often repeats simple phrases.

Rock = To move your body back and forth or from side to side in a swaying motion.

Knees Knockin' = To move your knees together and apart several times.

The Body Rock *Activities*

One Body-Part Rock:

Everybody spread out so that each of you has plenty of room to move. Play the music and begin by "rocking" just your hands. Move your hands high and low, fast and slow and all around. Now "rock" just your arms and move them all around. Try moving your arms many different ways. Keep going until you have "rocked" each part of your body, including your shoulders, chest, stomach, hips, legs, knees, feet, and head.

Music: Section A

Whole Body Rock:

Now you get to "rock" your whole body in all sorts of ways. Move side to side, front to back, high and low and all around. Remember to move each part of your body while you do the *Whole Body Rock.*

Music: Section B B1

Two Body-Part Rock:

Spread out and begin by "rocking" two parts of your body at a time. Start with your arms and legs. Then try your elbows and knees, your head and stomach, your shoulders and hips and your hands and feet. Choose as many different pairs of body parts of which you can think.

The Body Rock

5. Ev'rybody rock your body from side to side,
   side to side, from side to side;
   come on, rock your body from side to side,
   doin' the body rock.

6. Come on rock your body from the front to the back,
   the front to the back, from the front to the back;
   well, come on rock your body from the front to the back,
   we're doin' the body rock.

   (to Coda ending)

The Body Rock Lesson Plan

Focus: *To learn the concept of directions and the vocabulary of body parts while warming-up the muscles.*

Objectives

- To increase understanding of body part identification.
- To develop strength, coordination and agility.
- To learn the concept of directions.
- To develop creativity.
- To increase endurance.
- To build a movement vocabulary.
- To develop better listening and following directions skills.

Procedure:

1) Have the children spread out so that everyone has enough room to move.
2) Turn to the beginning of the chapter and do the activities that match the music in *One Body-Part Rock* and *Whole Body Rock*.
3) Play *THE BODY ROCK* and encourage the children to sing-along as you join them in this dance.

Reinforcing Positive Behavior:

When the children are moving the body part that the song dictates.

''I like that you are listening so carefully to the lyric and moving the correct body parts!''

When each child is moving a specified body part differently.

''Look how you are all moving your arms in a different way!''

When the children are enthusiastically participating.

''I like how you're smiling and putting lots of good energy into this dance!''

Handling Possible Problems:

Some of the children may not be listening to the lyric and following directions.

Compliment the children who are listening well and mention that you know the rest of the group can too.

Some of the children may say that they are feeling ''tired.''

If the children are genuinely exhausted or not feeling well, allow them to sit down and rest. Some children say they are tired when, in fact, they are feeling something else. They may just need some attention. Talk to those children. Try to find out how they are feeling. Ask them if they would like to pick a special place in the room, next to a good friend, to dance. Give them something special to do, like turning the pages of the book, or going around and making sure everyone has enough room to move.

The Freeze *Moving and "Freezing" Activities*

The Purpose:

THE FREEZE gives children the opportunity to do free-style dancing. Body control develops as children learn to stop moving and hold still the moment they hear the music stop. In addition to being lots of fun, *THE FREEZE* builds endurance and is an excellent aerobic activity.

Kids' Glossary

Freeze = To stop moving and hold your body as still as you can.

The Freeze *Activities*

Dance and Freeze with Me:

The leader will play and stop the music. The rest of you choose a partner. When the music starts to play, start dancing with your partner. The moment the music stops, you stop. When the music comes on again, switch partners and start dancing again. Each time the music stops, you "freeze." When the music comes on again, you change partners and dance. Continue until you've danced with several different people.

Music: Do this activity throughout the entire song.

Dance and Freeze:

Play *THE FREEZE* or other music that you like. If the song you choose does not have built in "freezes," have the leader play and stop the music at different intervals. The moment you hear the music start, you dance. Move your whole body all around the room. The moment you hear the music stop, you stop! Dance and Freeze for a few minutes until you all feel you've had a good work out.

Music: Do this activity throughout the entire song.

Freeze Dance:

Half of you spread out in the room and make your bodies into one of your favorite shapes and hold still (let's call you Group 1). The rest of you (let's call you Group 2) get to dance around your friends as they hold their bodies perfectly still. The moment the music stops, Group 2 stops and "freezes." The moment the music comes back on, Group 2 stays still, and then Group 1 gets to dance around all the "frozen" people in Group 2. Continue until each group has danced several times.

Music: Do this activity throughout the entire song.

Move and Freeze:

Once again the leader will play and stop the music. Begin by calling out different parts of the body for everyone to move: Start with the hands. Ask everyone to move their hands all around and the moment the music stops, everyone "freezes." Then call out "arms." Continue until you have experienced moving and "freezing" each part of your body.

Music: Do this activity throughout the entire song.

The Freeze

Words and Music by GREG SCELSA

Medium Rock Beat

(1.) Now here's a game that's kind-a' neat, just get your bod-y in the

(2.) *Instrumental*

beat. But when you hear the mus-ic quit,_____ don't wan-na see you move a

bit._____ Now you can dance an-y way that you please,_____

1. but lis-ten close-ly for the freeze. *(Freeze)*

2. freeze. *(Freeze)*

Now you can hop and you can bop, and you can flip and you can flop, and you can

rock and roll with style and ease; and you can bump and you can hus-tle, but don't

ev-er move a mus-cle when you hear the mus-ic come in-to the freeze. *(Freeze)*

The Freeze *Lesson Plan*

Focus: *To develop body control and an individual style of moving from an aerobic activity.*

Objectives:

- To explore different ways of moving and free-style dancing.
- To learn how to stop moving when the music stops.
- To build muscles and increase endurance.
- To develop a sense of rhythm.
- To dance harmoniously as a group.
- To develop body awareness and control.
- To build a movement vocabulary.
- To develop creativity.

Procedure:

1) Have everyone find their own space in the room. Do this by having each person find a spot in the room and ask them to spread their arms out to either side. If each person is not touching anyone as they sway their arms around, they have found their own space and have enough room to move.
2) Turn to *Dance And Freeze* at the beginning of the chapter and play *THE FREEZE* as you and the children dance.
3) For variation you can play *THE FREEZE* and do *Dance And Freeze With Me, Freeze Dance* or *Move And Freeze.*

Reinforcing Positive Behavior:

When the children are moving differently.
"I like how you are all moving in your own special way!"

When the children are utilizing all the space around them.
"You are moving all around the room, that's great!"

When the children stop the moment the music stops.
"You really know how to stop moving and hold your bodies perfectly still!"

Handling Possible Problems:

Some of the children may want to bump into each other as they dance.

Explain that it is not safe to bump bodies. This type of behavior may indicate that the children want to dance with partners. Ask if they would like to do *Dance And Freeze With Me.*

Some of the children may keep moving when the music stops.

Reinforce the positive behavior of those children who are keeping their bodies still when the music stops. Mention that you know that the rest of the group can "freeze" too. If they persist, and are disrupting everyone, you may want to give them a choice to either dance and follow directions or sit down until they feel ready to cooperate. **Note:** Very young children may have genuine difficulty holding their bodies still. However, with encouragement and continued practice, they will learn.

Some children may want to run all over the place.

Encourage the children to move their bodies in different ways. Offer some ideas. Call out different body parts to move, ask them to try twirling, jumping, skipping, etc. . .

Count Bounce *Learning Math Through Movement*

The Purpose:

COUNT BOUNCE helps children learn mathematics. By making number shapes with the body, children learn how to count, add, subtract, multiply and even divide. Making numbers with the body is fun and a creative way for children to master mathematical equations.

Kids' Glossary

Number Shape = To make the shape of a number with your body.

+ **The addition symbol** = To add up two or more numbers. For example: 2 + 2 = 4.

– **The subtraction symbol** = To take away one number from a larger number and end up with a smaller number. For example: 4 – 2 = 2.

÷ **The division symbol** = To separate out equal parts of a number. For example: 8 ÷ 2 = 4. This means that there are four sets of 2 in 8.

× **The multipication symbol** = To multiply is a quicker way of adding up numbers. For example: 3 × 3 = 9. This means that there are three sets of 3 in 9.

= **The equal symbol** = Whenever you add, subtract, divide or multiply any two numbers they always equal another number. For example: 5 + 3 = 8.

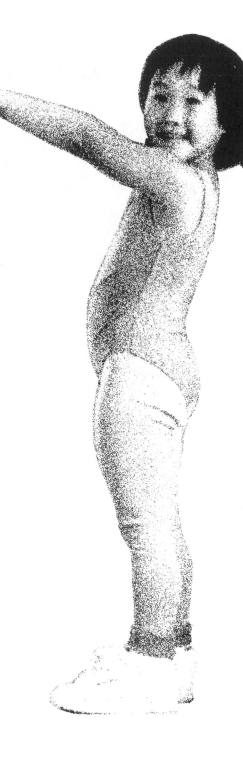

Count Bounce Activities

"1"   "2"

"11"   "12"

Note to Leader: *Make sure that the children can visualize numbers.*

Count To Ten:

Begin by writing out the numbers 1–10 on a chalkboard or on separate cards. You can also buy cards already printed from an educational supply store. Spread out so that each of you has plenty of room to move and make sure that everyone can see the numbers. Start with number "1." Everyone call out the number and make your bodies into the shape of it. Then, call out the number "2." Everyone call out that number and make your bodies into the shape of it. Continue until you have counted to 10. Try many different ways of making number shapes with your bodies.

Music: Section A

Count Past Ten:

This activity is excellent for children over five. Everyone get a partner. Have one of you show the number "11" on a card or chalkboard. Standing next to your partner, everyone call out that number and make the shapes. Now hold up the number "12" and you and your partner decide which of you will make the number "1" and which of you will make the number "2." Continue counting and making number shapes for as long as you wish. Remember to try different ways of making the numbers with your body. If you choose to go beyond the number "99," simply have everyone work in threes or fours, or however many people are needed to make the desired number!

Music: Play as instrumental.

The Count Bounce Dance:

Point to yourselves as you dance and sing the following lyric from the *COUNT BOUNCE* song:

"Hey, who's got the number?
We've got the number! We've got the number!
Hey, who's got the number?
We've got the number on the Count Bounce count-down!"

Music: Section B

Count Bounce Activities

"4 + 2 = 6"

"8 − 3 = 5"

The Adding Game:

This activity is excellent for children who know how or are learning to add: Sit in a large circle and one of you begins by entering the middle and making any number shape you'd like with your body. Call it out. The next person makes their body in the shape of "+." The next person calls out and makes another number shape with his/her body. The next person makes an "=" shape with his/her body, and then the next person (or people, depending on how many are needed) adds up the numbers and makes the final number shape with his/her body. Here is an example: 4 + 2 = 6. After you have decided what numbers to add, write them on a card or chalkboard. Continue until each of you has had a turn adding up the numbers and making the final number shape.

Music: Play as instrumental.

The Subtracting Game:

Do the same as above but subtract the numbers. For example: 8 - 3 = 5. Remember to write your equation on a card or chalkboard first. Continue until each of you has had a turn subtracting the numbers and making the final number shape with your body.

Music: Play as instrumental.

Count Bounce Activities

"7 × 1 = 7"

These next two activities are excellent for children who can multiply and divide:

The Multiplying Game:

Do the same as you did with adding and subtracting but this time multiply the numbers. For example: $7 \times 1 = 7$. Remember to write the numbers on a chalkboard or card before beginning. Continue until each of you has had the opportunity of calling out the answer and making the final number shape.

"8 ÷ 4 = 2"

The Dividing Game:

Do the same as above but divide the numbers. Here is an example: $8 \div 4 = 2$. Continue until each of you has had a chance to call out the answer and make the final number shape with your body.

Count Bounce

Moderate Shuffle with a bounce

"One!" That's the num-ber when I'm all a - lone; ___ a sin-gle scoop up-on my
"Five!" Of my fin-gers in a "high - five" hi; ___ put them up and then I

ice - cream cone. "Two!" That's the num-ber in a pair of shoes; ___
wave good - bye. ___ "Six!" Yum-my cook-ies in a half a doz - en;

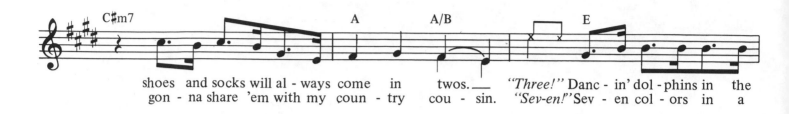

shoes and socks will al - ways come in twos.___ *"Three!"* Danc - in' dol - phins in the
gon - na share 'em with my coun - try cou - sin. *"Sev-en!"* Sev - en col - ors in a

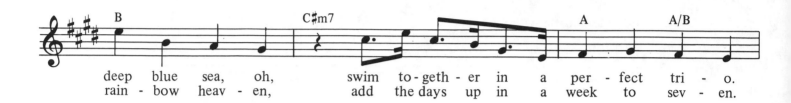

deep blue sea, oh, swim to-geth - er in a per - fect tri - o.
rain - bow heav - en, add the days up in a week to sev - en.

"Four!" Luck - y pet - als on a four - leaf clov - er; luck - y me I'm feel - ing
"Eight!" That's the time I have to go to bed;___ count the sheep a-jump-in'

good all o - ver.
o - ver - head.___ } Hey.___ Who's___ got___ the num - ber?

We've got___ the num - ber, we've___ got___ the num - ber. Hey,___ who's_

___ got___ the num - ber? We've___ got___ the num-ber on the Count Bounce count-down.

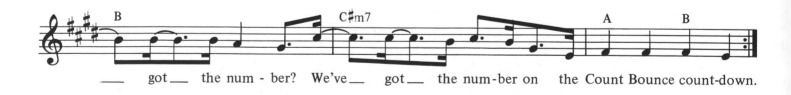

"Nine!" It's like a six but it's up - side down;___ that's the num-ber of the

Words and Music by KEVIN QUINN, CAROL QUINN, DONALD QUINN and LEE GARLAND

Count Bounce clown.__ *"Ten!"* Num- ber ten will take a one and ze - ro;

count a-gain and be the Count Bounce he - ro. *"One!"* *"Three!"* *"Five!"* *"Seven!"*

Play 4 times
Shout:
Bass

"Two!" *"Four!"* *"Six!"* *"Eight!"*

"Nine!" It's like a six but it's up - side down.__ *"Ten!"* Snap your fin - gers and you

turn a - round.__ Hey,__ who's__ got__ the num - ber!

We've got__ the num - ber, we've__ got__ the num - ber. Hey,_____ show_

_____ me __ the num - ber. We've__ got __ the num-ber on the Count Bounce count-down. Hey,__

Repeat and Fade

25

Count Bounce *Lesson Plan*

Focus: *Counting and making number shapes with the body.*

Objectives:

- To discover different ways of making number shapes with the body.
- To develop creativity and imagination.
- To learn mathematics in an enjoyable way.
- To strengthen mind/body coordination.

Procedure:

1) Ask the children to spread out so that everyone has enough room to move.
2) Write the numbers 1–10 on a chalkboard or place the number cards on something so they are visible to everyone.
3) Point to each number and ask the children to count out loud.
4) Turn to the beginning of the chapter and do *Count To Ten* with the children.
5) Turn to *The Count Bounce Dance* and practice the movements with the children.
6) Play the music for *COUNT BOUNCE* as you and the children do the movements and sing the words. Remember to keep the number cards visible.

Reinforcing Positive Behavior:

When the children are thinking of different ways to make one specific number.

"Look at all the different ways of making the number 6."

When the children are singing and dancing to the words in the chorus.

"I like how everyone is pointing to themselves and singing when the lyrics say, 'We've got the number, we've got the number!'"

Handling Possible Problems:

Some of the children may feel that this activity is too hard.

Tell these children that you understand and at first it is a little hard. Do it slowly. Just learn a few numbers a day until everyone feels ready to dance the song. Making number shapes gets easier with continued practice.

The World Is a Rainbow *Quiet Time*

The Purpose:

THE WORLD IS A RAINBOW is a beautiful song and a meaningful topic of conversation for a rest period. After body movement, children enjoy sitting quietly with their friends. It is a special time to sing and talk about the world we all share.

The World Is a Rainbow *Activities*

Sitting comfortably on the floor, after drinking some water, listen to THE WORLD IS A RAINBOW. Then discuss the following questions with the group. After hearing the first question, one of you at a time answers, and then goes on to the next question. (To enhance this activity, bring in pictures of nature, city and country life, animals and people from different parts of the world.)

Reflection and Discussion:

Close your eyes for a moment and think about the world. Think about nature, animals, cities, and the different people who live all over the world.

- If you could do anything, what would you like to do?
- If you could go anywhere, where would you like to go?
- What do different people do during the day? For example: Your mom and dad, sister and brother, grandmother and grandfather, your teacher, a fireperson, a doctor, a dentist or a postperson?
- What is in a city?
- What are parts of nature that share our world? Like, trees, flowers, mountains, rivers, plants, waterfalls, etc. . . Can you think of any others?
- What are different animals that live in the world?
- What do you feel is most special about the world?

The World Is a Rainbow

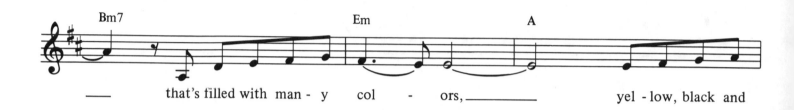

The world is a rain - bow,

— that's filled with man - y col - ors, yel - low, black and

white, and brown, you see them all a - round. The world is a

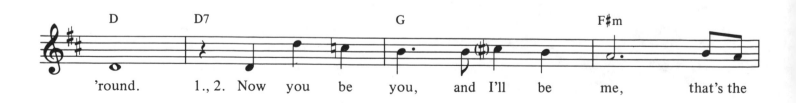

rain - bow, with man - y kinds of peo - ple.
(2.) (La - la - la . . . .)

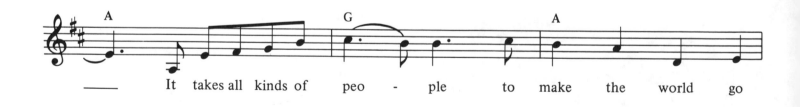

— It takes all kinds of peo - ple to make the world go

'round. 1., 2. Now you be you, and I'll be me, that's the

way we were meant to be._____ But the world is a mix-ing

cup, just look what hap-pens when you stir it up.

The world_ is a rain - bow,_____ with man-y kinds of

peo - ple,_____ and when we work to-geth - er, it's

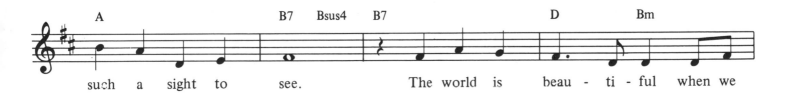

such a sight to see. The world is beau-ti-ful when we

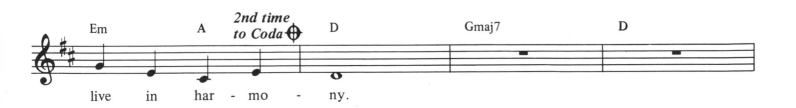

live in har - mo - ny.

La la la la la,

ny.   *La, la, etc.*

The Purpose:

THE BALANCING ACT is a series of postures that develop concentration and body control. Strength and flexibility increase as children learn to balance in these sustained positions.

Kids' Glossary

Postures = Special balancing positions.

Balance = To divide your weight equally in different positions.

Rooted = *Roots* are the underground part of a tree. Imagine that your feet are *rooted* into the ground keeping you firmly in place.

"Shift Your Weight" = To put all of your weight onto one leg so that you can lift your other leg and balance.

Forward/Backward = *Forward* means to move to the front and *backward* means to move to the back.

Raise/Lower = *Raise* is to lift something up and *lower* means to bring it down.

Spread = To open and stretch out.

Extend = To reach or stretch a body part.

Squat = To lower your body so that your knees are bent and your bottom nearly touches the heels of your feet and the ground.

Left = Everything to the side of your body in which your heart is located.

Right = Everything to the side of your body which is away from your heart.

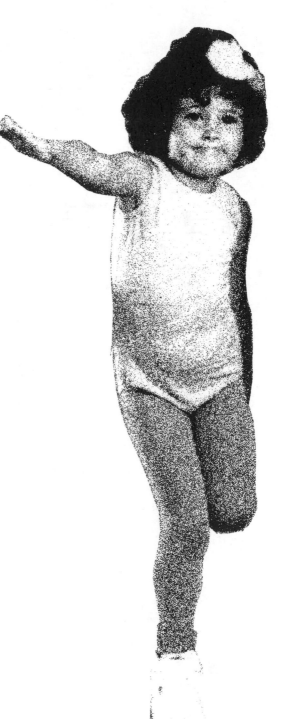

Point To These Body Parts

- Ankle
- Palms
- Balls of feet
- Heels
- Fingertips

The Postures

The Tall Giraffe:

Standing tall with legs slightly apart, place your arms straight down in front of your body and let your palms face the floor. Gently stretch your neck, lift your head, and come up on to the balls of your feet. Balance in *The Tall Giraffe* for several seconds, lower your heels, and then try it again.

Music: Section A

The Cuckoo Bird:

Stand with your legs wide apart and bend your upper body forward. Raise your arms straight up behind you with palms down and lift up your head. With legs straight, slowly lift your heels up and balance on the balls of your feet. Hold this position for several seconds, lower your heels and then try the *Cuckoo Bird* again.

Music: Section B

The Mountain:

Standing with your legs wide apart, stretch your arms up high above you and place your palms together. Lift your heels off the ground and balance on the balls of your feet. Hold this position for several seconds, lower your heels, and then try *The Mountain* again.

Music: Section C

The Balancing Act Activities

The Archer's Bow:

Stand with your legs slightly apart and shift your weight onto the left leg. Bend and lift your right leg behind you. Hold onto your right foot with your right hand and extend your left arm out in front of your body. Bend your upper body forward and gently pull your right bent leg up as high as you can. Balance in this position for several seconds. Then, let go of your foot and stand with both feet on the ground again. Now try *The Archer's Bow* on your other leg.

Music: Section A1

The Arrow:

Stand tall with your feet close together and raise your arms high above your head. Hold your hands together. Lift up your heels and balance on the balls of your feet for several seconds. Lower your heels and then do *The Arrow* again.

Music: Section B1

The Easy Chair:

Stand with your legs slightly apart and extend your arms out straight in front of your body. Slowly lower your body by bending your knees and raising your heels. Balance in this position for several seconds. Lower your heels, return to the original standing postion and do *The Easy Chair* again.

Music: Section C1

The Balancing Act *Activities*

The Banana Boat:

Laying on your stomach with legs, arms and head lifted, reach back and hold your feet. Rock back and forth for several seconds. Let go of your feet, rest on your stomach with your legs, arms and head on the floor and then try *The Banana Boat* again.

Music: Section D

The Circus Ball:

Sit on your bottom with your arms wrapped tightly around bent legs. Lift your feet off the floor and balance on your bottom. Hold this position for several seconds. Place your feet on the ground and then try the *Circus Ball* again.

Music: Section D1

The Greeting:

Sit on your bottom with arms wrapped around bent legs. Tuck your head in close to your knees. On the count of three lift your arms and legs and wave "Hi!" to your friends with your feet and hands. Try to keep your arms and legs straight. After a few seconds come back to the original position and tuck in your head. Repeat *The Greeting* several times, each time balancing on your bottom with straight legs and arms.

Music: Section E

The Balancing Act Activities

The Tree:

Standing tall, shift your weight to one leg. Place your lifted foot on the inner side of your standing leg, by the ankle or knee, and raise your arms high, as if they were branches on a tree. Try several different ways of stretching, twisting and hanging your arms. Imagine that your feet are rooted into the ground like a tree, holding you firmly in place, and your arms are like the many different branches. Hold this shape for several seconds, changing your arm positions, and then do *The Tree* on the other leg.

Music: Play as instrumental

The Star:

Stand tall with your legs wide apart and lift your arms diagonally above you. Raise your heels and balance on the balls of your feet. Hold this position for several seconds, lower your heels and do *The Star* again.

Music: Play as instrumental

The Elephant:

Standing with your legs slightly apart, hold your hands together in front of your body. Slowly shift your weight to one leg and lift and bend your other leg behind you. Bend your upper body forward. Hold this position for several seconds and then try *The Elephant* on the other leg. Remember to think about the heaviness of this animal.

Music: Play as instrumental

The Balancing Act Activities

The Bumble Bee:

Stand tall with your legs slightly apart and let your arms hang by your sides. Shift your weight to one leg. Lift and raise your other leg back and up while bending your upper body forward—let your arms go back and up too. Lift your leg as high as you can while balancing several seconds in this position. Lower your leg and then try The *Bumble Bee* with the other leg.

Music: Play as instumental

The Pretzel:

Stand tall and shift your weight over to one leg. Wrap your other leg around your standing leg and twist your arms together. Balance in this position for several seconds, untwist and then do *The Pretzel* again, shifting your weight to the other leg. Try twisting your body a different way each time.

Music: Play as instrumental

The Spider:

Squatting with your feet wide apart, place your fingertips on the floor in front of your body. Raise your heels and balance on the balls of your feet and fingertips. Now, try to shift your weight from one leg to the other while moving your fingertips around the floor in front of you. Balance in *The Spider* for several seconds, shifting your weight from leg to leg. Think about how a spider moves.

Music: Play as instrumental

The Balancing Act

arms down low and stretch your neck up high;
one leg be-hind you and stretch it so;

like a tall gi-raffe with his head in the sky.
you do your best ren-di-tion of an arch-er's bow. Yeah.

Then bend your bod-y down and put your
Now put your hands up skin-ny top,

arms back flat,
legs in tight.

just like a cuck-oo bird or a
Stand on your tip-py toes.and you're an

sup-er jet, yeah.
ar-row in flight.

Now spread your legs out wide,
Now sit like an eas-y chair,

point-ing your hands up high.
e-ven though noth-ing's there.

Make a moun-tain like
Put your hands in your

that
lap
in the bal-anc-ing act.
in the bal-anc-ing act.

Now grab
Now lay
face down, grab your feet,
sit up, make your-self

don't let go,
real small,
and you'll
and you'll

soon be do-in' the ba - nan - a boat.
wind up look-in' like a cir-cus ball. Yeah.

Now
Put your arms and your legs out straight.

Wave good-bye 'cause we're run-ning late.
It's been fun, hur-ry

back
knack
to the bal-anc-ing act.
for the bal-anc-ing act.

'Cause we all got the

The Balancing Act *Lesson Plan*

Focus: To learn how to balance in different positions.

Objectives:

- To learn to focus, concentrate and balance.
- To develop body control.
- To increase flexibility, strengthen muscles and develop coordination.

Procedure:

1) Form a large circle with the children.
2) Turn to the beginning of the chapter and practice the activities that match the music.
3) Play the music for THE BALANCING ACT. Do the postures with the children and encourage them to sing-along.

Reinforcing Positive Behavior:

When the children are listening and paying attention.

"I like how everyone is listening so well and saving their talking for later."

When the children are concentrating and balancing well.

"You're doing great at balancing. I can see that you are all really trying!"

Handling Possible Problems:

If some children are talking.

Explain that it is much easier to balance and concentrate if they don't talk.

Some children may feel that balancing is too hard for them.

Tell them that you understand and that they are doing very well. Remind the children to do the best they can and that balancing will get easier the more they practice.

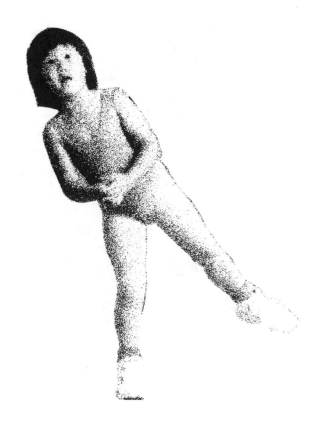

Beanbag Boogie *Beanbag Activities I & II*

The Purpose:

BEANBAG BOOGIE is a series of activities that strengthen children's sense of balance while developing body part identification and coordination. These activities increase children's metabolic rate and help develop their cardiovascular system.

Kids' Glossary

March = To walk in a line with other people counting 1, 2, 3, 4 over and over again.

Shake = To move in a quick and jerky manner.

Stomp = To pound your feet on the ground.

Rock = To sway your body back and forth or from side to side.

Point To These Body Parts

- Back
- Calf
- Thigh
- Chest

Note To Leader: All of the activities in this chapter require beanbags. If you do not have any, they are very easy to make. Simply take two squares of cloth, sew three sides together, fill the pouch with beans and then sew the last side together.

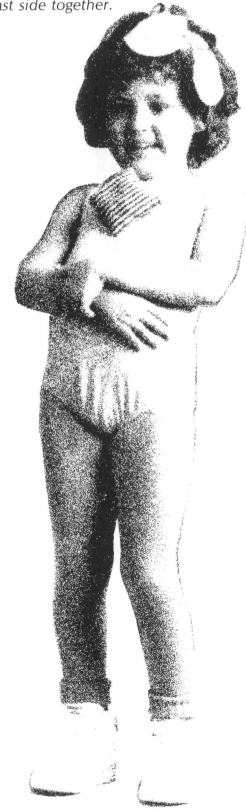

Beanbag Boogie *Activities*

Beanbag Moves:

Place the beanbag on your head and slowly move around the room—try to keep it from falling! Then, put the beanbag on your shoulder and walk around the room. Ask one person at a time to suggest a body part on which to balance the beanbag. Put it on your elbow, hand, forehead, finger, ear, tummy, back, knee, arm, nose, wrist, foot, leg and chest. Place the beanbag under your chin, under your arm and between your knees. Explore many ways of moving while balancing the beanbag on different body parts.

Music: Sections A, A1, A2

Beanbag Balance:

Place the beanbag on one part of your body at a time for several seconds. Keep your body very still and try to keep it from falling. Start with the beanbag on your head, then one shoulder and then ask someone what body part the beanbag can be placed on next. Continue asking for suggestions until the beanbag has been placed on every part of your body. Put it on your elbow, hand, finger, nose, cheek, ear, tummy, back, hip, arm, thigh, foot, knee, calf and chest.

Beanbag Boogie:

Do this in the chorus of the *BEANBAG BOOGIE song or with any terrific rock music you like,* and get ready to dance with your beanbag. Hold it in your hand as you try many different ways of moving, such as jumping, stomping, shaking, twisting and rocking.

Music: Section B

Beanbag Freeze:

Once again, choose some music to which you would like to dance. The leader can start and stop the music on the piano or turn on and off the record or tape player at various intervals. One of you call out a body part on which the beanbag will be placed when the music stops. Dance to the music with your beanbag in your hand. The moment the music stops, place the beanbag on the body part that was called out. Try to keep your body perfectly still. Continue dancing and stopping until you have placed the beanbag on many different body parts.

Beanbag March:

One of you lead the others in this marching activity by placing the beanbag on one part of your body and marching around the room. Everyone else places the beanbag on the same body part and follows you in a line. Then, go to the end of the line and the next person leads by placing the beanbag on a different body part and marching around the room in a different direction. Continue marching with knees lifted high until everyone has had a turn leading. Try Greg and Steve's *"Friendship March"* or *"Muffin Man."*

Beanbag Pass:

Form a circle with your friends. One of you begin by thinking of a special way to pass the beanbag to the person next to you. Start by passing it between your legs. Your neighbor takes the beanbag and then passes it in the same way to the person next to him/her, until everyone has had a turn. Then, another person begins by thinking of a different way to pass the beanbag. Continue passing the beanbag until each of you has had a turn leading a pass.

Suggestions for Beanbag Pass:

1) Over the head
2) Under an arm
3) Under one lifted leg
4) Balancing on a body part
   (elbow, shoulder, finger etc. . .)

Beanbag Boogie Activities

Beanbag Catch #1:

Stand up straight and gently throw the beanbag in the air. Try to catch it as it falls down. Practice throwing and catching the beanbag by yourself several times. Remember to watch the beanbag as it goes up and down.

Beanbag Catch #2

Now try throwing and catching the beanbag with a friend. First stand a little apart and then back up a few steps and try it standing further apart. Remember to keep your eye on the beanbag and throw it gently.

Beanbag Catch #3

Form a big circle with your friends. Have one person start by throwing a beanbag to the person next to him/her. That person will then throw the beanbag to the person next to him/her, until everyone has had a turn throwing and catching. Then, have one person call out a friend's name anywhere in the circle to whom to throw the beanbag. Then, the person who catches it will call someone else's name and throw the beanbag to him/her. Continue throwing the beanbag until everyone has had several turns.

Beanbag Kick #1

Place the beanbag on the floor and begin by *gently* kicking it around the room. First kick the beanbag several times with one foot and then try it several times with your other foot.

Beanbag Kick #2

Pick a partner and *gently* kick the beanbag back and forth to each other several times with each foot.

Beanbag Boogie I

bean - bag on your { el - bow,___ and move your bod-y to___ the
ear,_____ and let the mus-ic make_you
knee.____ Can you boog-ie? Boog-ie all a -

sound._____ Yay, yeah._____ }
move. _____ Woe, whoa._____ }
round._____ Yay, yeah._____ }

B B1 B2

Now hold that bean-bag in your hand_ and boog-ie while_you can._Come on_ and

Chorus:

{Jump } to the bean - bag boog - ie.____ { Come on___ and
{Shake } Ev - 'ry - bod - y
{Stomp } Ev - 'ry - bod - y

jump } to the bean - bag boog - ie.__ { Ev -'ry-bod-y jump }to the bean - bag
shake } Let me see you shake }
stomp } Stomp your feet now, ba-by }

Fine 3rd time

boog - ie. __ { Come on_ and jump }to the bean - bag boog - ie.__ 2. Put your
Ev-'ry-bod - y shake_} 3. Put that
Um, come on_ and stomp }

45

Beanbag Boogie II

Put your beanbag on your arm
While you move your body to the sound.

Now put your beanbag on your nose;
Don't let your beanbag touch the ground.

Now put your beanbag on your wrist,
And move your body all around.

Now hold that beanbag in your hand,
And boogie while you can.

Come on and rock to the Beanbag Boogie.
Everybody rock to the Beanbag Boogie.
Everybody rock to the Beanbag Boogie.
Rock your body *(boogie)* to the Beanbag Boogie.

Put your beanbag on your foot
While you move any way you choose.

Now put your beanbag on your leg,
And get your whole self in the groove.

Now put your beanbag on your chest,
And let the music make you move. Yeah, yeah.

Now hold that beanbag in your hand,
And boogie while you can.

Come on and twist to the Beanbag Boogie.
Make your body twist to the Beanbag Boogie.
Show me how you twist to the Beanbag Boogie.
Everybody twist to the Beanbag Boogie.

Put that beanbag under your chin,
And rock, boogie to the sound.

Put that beanbag under your arm;
Remember, don't let it touch the ground.

Now put your beanbag between your knees,
And boogie, boogie all around. Yeah, yeah.

Now hold that beanbag in your hand;
Boogie while you can.

Come on and dance to the Beanbag Boogie.
Show me how you dance to the Beanbag Boogie.
Boogie all around to the Beanbag Boogie.
Come on, baby, boogie to the Beanbag Boogie.

Beanbag Boogie *Lesson Plan*

Focus: To teach children how to balance a beanbag on different body parts while moving.

Objectives:

- To strengthen body part identification.
- To learn to balance a beanbag on different body parts.
- To develop coordination and a sense of rhythm.
- To provide an aerobic activity and strengthen the cardiovascular system.
- To build a movement vocabulary.
- To feel a sense of joy and comfort from moving and dancing with peers.

Procedure:

1) Give each child a beanbag.
2) Have the children spread out so that everyone has enough room to move.
3) Do the activities that match the music from *Beanbag Moves* and *Beanbag Rock*.
4) Play the music for *BEANBAG BOOGIE I* as you and the children dance and sing-along.
5) Next time, play the music for *BEANBAG BOOGIE II* as you join the children in this dance.

Reinforcing Positive Behavior:

When the children are balancing the beanbag on different body parts properly.

"You are all balancing your beanbags so well!"

When the children find different ways of moving while placing the beanbag on a specific body part.

"Look how everyone is moving in different ways!"

When the children pick up their beanbags when they fall.

"I like how you pick up the beanbags when they fall and continue listening and moving!"

Handling Possible Problems:

Some children may want to throw their beanbags at inappropriate times.

Explain to the children that now they are using their beanbags for balancing and dancing. Tell them that they will be able to throw their beanbags during the *Beanbag Catch*.

Some children may feel frustrated if their beanbags fall.

Explain to the children that it's okay if their beanbag falls. Show them that your beanbag falls sometimes too and that you just pick it up and keep on going.

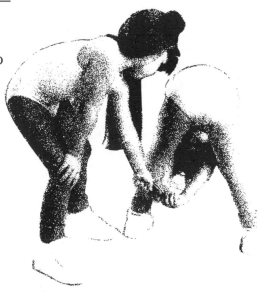

Body Talk *Advanced Warm-Ups and Stretches*

The Purpose:

BODY TALK is a series of exercises and isolated body part movements that teach children how to properly warm-up their muscles. Strength and flexibility are developed through gentle stretching, and body control is enhanced as children learn to move one part of their body at a time.

Kids' Glossary

Posture = Good posture is when you stand-up tall and straight.

Muscle = Body tissue that supports your bones and allows you to move around.

Warm-ups= Special exercises that you do to flex and stretch the muscles that help prevent you from feeling sore.

Flex = To bend and stretch the muscles.

Stretch = To gently pull and lengthen the muscles.

Point to these body parts:

- Eyebrows
- Eyes
- Nose
- Cheeks
- Mouth
- Tongue
- Chin
- Head
- Shoulders
- Elbows
- Hands
- Fingers
- Arms
- Chest
- Stomach
- Hips
- Legs
- Knees
- Feet

Body Talk Activities

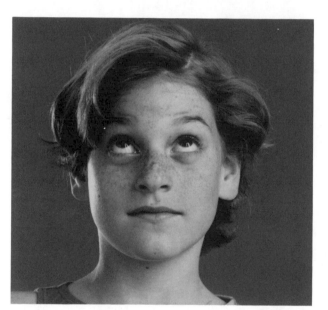

Note to Leader: *Play any moderate tempo music as you and the children do the following activities.*

Perfect Posture:

Stand tall with your legs and feet a little apart, push your shoulders back, hold your tummies and bottoms in, and let your arms hang by your sides. Remember to breathe; inhale through your nose and exhale through your mouth.

THE WARM-UPS:

Get ready to move one part of your body at a time, from your eyebrows to your feet!

Eyebrows:

Standing in your best posture, begin by moving your eyebrows only. . . up and down and up and down.

Lyric: Section A

Eyes:

Now move your eyes. Try to keep the rest of your body still as you move your eyes all around. Look up and down and side to side. Do you see your friends looking all around too as they keep the rest of their bodies still?

Body Talk *Activities*

Nose:

Move your nose now, like a bunny!

Lyric: Section B

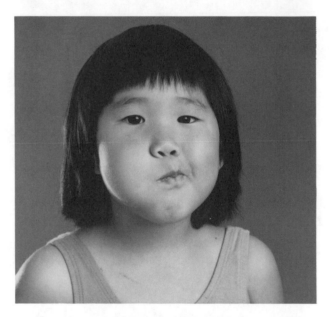

Cheeks:

Now move your cheeks. puff them like a frog!

Lyric: Section C

Mouth:

Can you move your mouth and make funny shapes with your lips?

Tongue:

Now move your tongue. . . like a lizard!

Lyric: Section D

Body Talk Activities

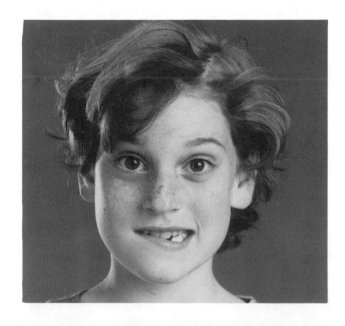

Chin:

What about your chin? Can you move your chin from side to side?

Lyric: Section E

Head:

Move your head. Slowly move your head down. And slowly move your head up. Try it again. Now move your head to the side and now the other side. Can you gently roll your head in a circle? Now try it in the opposite direction?

Lyric: Section F

Shoulders:

Now warm-up your shoulders. Move them up and down and up and down. Can you move your shoulders in circles? How about the other direction? What other ways can you move your shoulders?

Lyric: Section G

Body Talk Activities

Elbows:

Try moving your elbows in several different ways. Around and around and up and down. You can even move them in a squiggly way!

Lyric: Section H

Hands:

Move your hands now. Can you wave "hello" to all your friends?

Lyric: Section I

Fingers:

Can you wiggle your fingers and gently tickle a friend?

Arms:

Now warm-up your arms. Swing them up and down, around in a circle, any way you'd like. Reach up real high and stretch.

Lyric: Section J

Body Talk *Activities*

Chest:

Let your arms help you move your chest out and in and out and in. Try it several times.

Lyric: Section K

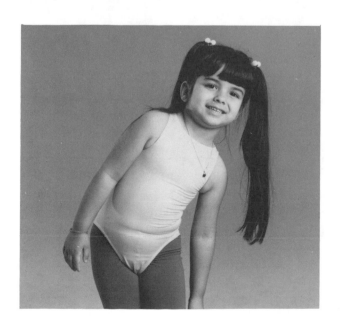

Stomach:

Can you move your stomach out and now in? Try it again a few times. Now try moving your stomach to the side and then to the other side? It's a little hard, but the more you practice the easier it will get.

Lyric: Section L

Hips:

Here's one that's fun. Move your hips from side to side and front to back a few times. Can you move your hips in a circle? Now try it the other way.

Lyric: Section M

Body Talk Activities

Legs:

Now, move one leg at a time. Stand tall, balance on one leg with your other leg lifted and arms extended out to your sides to help you balance. Gently swing your lifted leg back and forth a few times, trying to balance on your standing leg. Try it with your other leg now. Swing it back and forth a few times. Remember to keep your standing leg straight.

Lyric: Section N

Knees:

Can you wiggle your knees together and apart several times? What other ways can you move your knees?

Lyric: Section O

Feet:

Standing on one leg again, with arms extended to your sides, point and flex the lifted foot in front of your body. Now flex and point to the side of your body and now to the back. Now, try the same thing with your other foot! Wiggle that foot to the front, to the side and then to the back.

Lyric: Section P

Body Talk Activities

Whole Body:

Now shake out your whole body; jump and wiggle every part of you!

Lyric: Section Q

THE STRETCHES:

The Body Stretch:

With your legs a little apart, reach your arms up high above you and stretch. Reach and stretch with one arm and then the other arm. Do *The Body Stretch* several times with each arm.

The Tent:

Stand with your legs a little apart and stretch your arms up high. Hold your hands together, lift up your heels and stand on the balls of your feet. Stay in this position for a few seconds. Now bring your heels down and repeat *The Tent* a couple more times.

Body Talk Activities

The Bridge:

With your legs apart and arms stretched up high, slowly bring your arms down, keeping your back straight, until your hands touch the ground and your body forms a big bridge. Do not force your legs to be straight. Just do the best you can, and with practice you will soon be able to do *The Bridge* with straight legs.

The Toe Touch:

Standing tall with your legs together and arms stretched up high, slowly reach down with your back straight and try to touch your toes. Reach down as far as you can, keeping your legs straight. Hold this position for several seconds, and then bend your knees and slowly roll up to the standing position. Do *The Toe Touch* a few times, bending over with a straight back and rolling up with a rounded back. With continued practice, you will be able to touch your toes with great ease.

Tickle Toes:

Sitting with straight backs, soles of feet together and hands on your ankles, bend forward and try to tickle your toes with your nose. Stay in this position for a few seconds and then roll up to the straight back position. Do *Tickle Toes* about four times.

The Sun Stretch:

Sitting with arms and legs wide open, feet up and backs straight, gently reach arms over and place both hands on one leg or foot. Try to keep both legs straight as you stretch as far as you are able. Then, slowly lift arms up and sway over to the other leg, gently stretching as far as you can while keeping both legs straight. Do *The Sun Stretch* several times slowly, swaying from leg to leg.

The Feet Party:

Everyone sit up tall in a circle together with legs straight and feet touching. Stretch arms up high above you and clap your hands. Then, slowly bring arms down and clap the bottoms of your feet with your hands. Try to keep your legs straight throughout *The Feet Party*. If you are not yet able to reach your feet, clap your knees or ankles, remembering to keep your legs straight. With practice you will soon be able to clap your feet!

The Slide:

Sitting tall with your legs straight and feet pointed, place your hands on the floor behind you, with fingers pointed away from your body. Lift your bottom while keeping your legs and arms straight (in the shape of a slide) and look up. Hold this position for several seconds and then gently lower your bottom back to the ground. Do *The Slide* a few more times, remembering to keep your legs and arms straight.

The Tortoise:

Sitting tall with your legs open and bent, place your hands on the floor in front of your body. Slowly slide each hand under each bent leg and bend your upper body forward so that your head gently touches the floor. Hold this position for a few seconds and then return to the upright sitting position. Practice doing *The Tortoise* a few more times.

The Kissing Cobra:

Lying on your stomach with legs straight and feet pointed, place your hands under your shoulders with palms down. Slowly press down on your hands and lift your upper body to a straight arm position. Stretch your neck up, look up and kiss. Slowly bend your arms, lower your back and return to the beginning position. Do *The Kissing Cobra* a few more times.

Body Talk Activities

The Baby Pose:

Sit on your knees with straight backs. Place your hands on the floor in front of your body and stretch out forward until your forehead is resting on the floor and your arms are straight. Rest in *The Baby Pose* for several seconds.

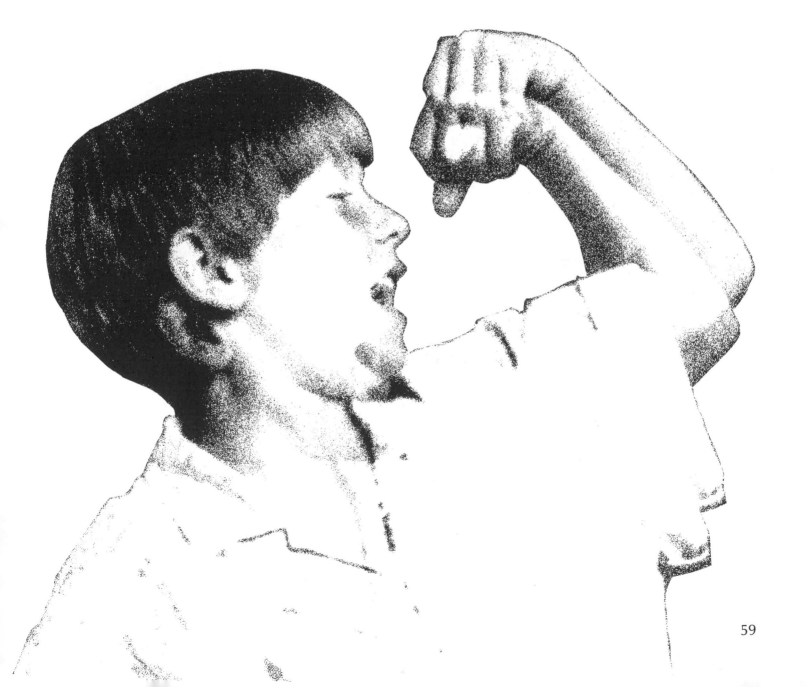

Body Talk Instruction Lyric

by Julie Weissman

Get ready to warm-up all the muscles in your body, everyone. All right! Let's get moving!

A. Move your eyebrows up and down.

B. Everybody move your nose. Like a bunny.

C. Move your cheeks. Like a frog.

D. Now move your mouth. Like a fish. Move your tongue like a lizard.

E. Move your chin. From side to side.

F. Now move your head around and around slowly.

G. Now move your shoulders up and down, up and down.

H. Now move your elbows. Wiggle those elbows.

I. Move your hands. Shake those hands. Everybody move your fingers. Make them wiggle.

J. Swing your arms. Swing them around and around.

K. Move your chest. In and out. Keep going. Good!

L. Now move your tummy. Stick it way out. Hold it in. Good work!

M. Now shake those hips. Warm-up those hips, from side to side. Move them around and around.

N. Move one leg. Swing it gently back and forth. Try to balance. Swing it slowly. Now the other leg. Try to balance. Swing it slowly. Good Work!

O. Move your knees. Wiggle those knees.

P. Now move one foot. Shake it all around. Get ready to shake your other foot. Move it all around. Shake it.

Q. All right. Get ready now. Shake your whole body out. Wiggle every part of you. Keep going! And Stop.

Give yourselves a hand everybody, you did a great job!

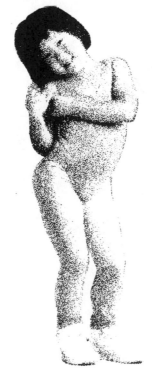

Body Talk *Lesson Plan*

Focus: *To teach the importance of properly warming-up and stretching the muscles before participating in other physical activities.*

Objectives:

- To develop body awareness, body control and body part identification.
- To strengthen muscles, increase flexibility and develop coordination.
- To build a movement vocabulary.
- To increase the ability to focus and concentrate.
- To learn to listen and follow directions.

Procedure:

1) Form a large circle with the children.
2) Turn to the beginning of this chapter and do The Warm-ups and the Stretches that match the lyric.

Reinforcing Positive Behavior:

When the children are standing in good posture.
"I like the way you are all standing so tall!"

When the children are listening and following directions.
"You are all listening and following directions so well!"

When the children are moving a particular body part in different ways.
"Look how you are all moving your arms in different ways, that's great!"

When the children are moving one body part at a time and keeping the rest of their bodies still.
"I like how you're keeping the rest of your bodies so still as you move just one body part at a time!"

When the children are keeping their legs straight while stretching.
"I like how you're keeping your legs straight and stretching only as far as you can!"

Handling Possible Problems:

Some of the children may be talking and disturbing the others.

Ask those children to please save their talking for later. Explain that this is a time to talk with their bodies and that they will be able to talk with their voices soon.

Children may want to move their whole body instead of one body part at a time.

Explain that, first, they are trying to keep their bodies very still while they move just one body part at a time. Mention that they will be able to move their whole bodies soon.

Some children may not feel ready to join in and may want to watch.

Allow those children to sit away from where the group is moving. Communicate that it is okay to watch, and that they can join in on this *fun* activity when they feel ready. Continually encourage them to participate.

Children may reinforce undesirable behavior.

For example: A small group of children may say, "We don't want to do this. This is stupid!" This may trigger the same reaction from some of the other children. You may want to give that group a choice to either join in with the rest of the children or sit quietly away from the activity. Or, if you have an assistant, he/she can do something else with those children during the movement session. Keep the feeling positive. If you force children to do something they don't want to do, it is harder for them to acquire a positive attitude about it.

Children may say, "This is too hard, I can't do this!!"

Explain to the children that some of the exercises are a little hard at first, but they get much easier with practice.

Some children have difficulty focusing and are easily distracted.

Direct an activity to those children as often as needed. For example: You may want to say, "Danny, let's move our noses now. Good job! You really know how to keep the rest of your body still while you move just your nose." Call out the names of those particular children who need help focusing. This technique strengthens children's ability to listen and concentrate.

Animal Action I & II
Shapes and Movements of Animals

The Purpose:

ANIMAL ACTION helps children learn creatively about the various shapes and movements of different animals. A sense of time, space, size and force is developed as children discover the unique qualities that exist in every living creature.

Kids' Glossary

Puff Out = To puff out your cheeks means to fill your mouth with air so that it pushes out your cheeks.

Note To Leader: *To enhance this activity take a trip to the zoo or share a picture book of animals with your group.*

Animal Action Activities

Animal Shapes:

Spread out so that each of you has plenty of room to move freely. One of you begins by calling out an animal for which everyone makes their bodies into the shape. For example: A frog—squat down low and puff out your cheeks.

Here are some other suggestions: Cat, snake, cow, giraffe, monkey, elephant, bunny, lion, horse, fish, octopus, spider, duck, bee and worm. Continue until you have made your body in the shape of many different animals.

Animal Movements:

Spread out again, so that everyone has enough room. One of you at a time call out an animal like which you want to move. For example: A bird—move your arms as if they were wings and run around the room. Try moving like many different animals using the suggestions above.

Music: Section B

Animal Action *Activities*

Animal Action Dance:

Part I: Make sure that each of you has plenty of room to move. Begin by singing and doing your favorite dancing to the chorus from the *ANIMAL ACTION* songs:

> "Animal Action
> It's so much fun,
> Animal Action
> Move like a. . . "

Music: Section A

Part 2: When you hear the words "Move like a. . . ," one of you at a time calls out an animal like which everyone can move. After everyone has moved like that animal for several seconds, sing the chorus again and someone else calls out an animal like which everyone can move. Continue until everyone has had a turn suggesting an animal.

Here is a list of the animals from the *ANIMAL ACTION* songs:

Elephant, cat, frog, bird, snake, horse, spider, bunny, lion, bee, duck and monkey.

Music: Section B

Animal Action Activities

Small Animals:

Now try moving like small animals. One of you begins by suggesting a small animal like which everyone could move. Move like as many different small animals of which you can think.

Here are some suggestions:
Fly, ant, squirrel, caterpillar, butterfly, kitten, hamster and fish.

Large Animals:

Now, try moving like large animals. Begin by one of you suggesting a large animal like which everyone can move.

Here are some suggestions:
Elephant, horse, cow, kangaroo, ape, whale, seal, bear, and hippopotamus.

Slow-Moving Animals:

Think about animals that usually move very slowly. One of you at a time suggest one like which everyone can move.

Here are some suggestions:
Turtle, worm, snail, elephant and caterpillar.

Fast-Moving Animals:

Each of you think about animals that can move fast. One of you at a time call out a fast-moving animal like which everyone can move.

Here are some suggestions:
Fox, dog, bird, squirrel, deer, horse and bumblebee.

Animal Action Game:

Sitting in a big circle, one of you at a time enter the center. Think about an animal like which you'd like to move. Do not say what it is, just start moving like it and try to make the sounds that that animal makes. Keep moving until someone guesses correctly the animal like which you are moving. Continue until each person in the group has had a turn moving like an animal.

Animal Action I & II

Animal Action I

Moderate, with a steady beat

Come on ev-'ry-bod-y, come down to the zoo.___ We're gon-na do a dance like the an-i-mals do.___ An-i-mal ac-tion it's so much fun.___ An-i-mal ac-tion, *Move like a horse.*

Giddyup! *(Woodblock sound)*

Giddyup!

Drum

An-i-mal ac-tion it's so much fun.___ An-i-mal ac-tion, *Move like a spi-der.*

69

Move like a bee.

An-i-mal ac-tion it's so much fun.____

An-i-mal ac-tion, *Move like a duck.*

An-i-mal ac-tion,

oo, oo, oo. _____ An - i - mal ac-tion.

Repeat and Fade

Animal Action II

Come

on ev - 'ry-bod-y, come down to the zoo. ___ We're gon-na do a dance like the

an - i -mals do. ___ An - i - mal ac - tion it's so much fun. _____

An - i - mal ac - tion, *Move like an el - e-phant.*

Drum

An - i - mal ac - tion it's so much fun. _____ An - i - mal ac - tion,

Move like a cat. Meow

Meow

An-i-mal ac-tion it's so much fun.

An-i-mal ac-tion, *Move like a frog.* Ribbet

Ribbet

Ribbet

An-i-mal ac-tion it's so much fun. An-i-mal ac-tion,

Move like a bird. Twittering sounds

Animal Action Lesson Plan

Focus: *To learn about and move like different animals.*

Objectives:

- To develop creativity and imagination.
- To strengthen mind/body coordination.
- To develop strength and endurance.
- To increase flexibility and agility.
- To learn the different ways animals move.

Procedure:

1) Sit comfortably on the carpet with the children.
2) Turn to *Animal Movements* at the beginning of the chapter.
3) Talk about the animals listed in the activity and make the appropriate sounds.
4) Find pictures of the animals to share with the children. (optional)
5) Ask the children to spread out so that everyone has enough room to move.
6) Practice the movements of the animals listed in *Animal Movements*.
7) Turn to *Animal Action Dance* and practice singing and dancing to the chorus.
8) Play the music for *ANIMAL ACTION I*. Encourage the children to make sounds as they move like each animal. Remember to sing and dance during the chorus.
9) Now, play the music for *ANIMAL ACTION II* as you and the children make the sounds, do the movements and sing-along.

Reinforcing Positive Behavior:

When the children discover different ways to move like a specific animal.''

''Look at all the different ways you can move like a bunny!''

When the children are singing and dancing during the chorus.

''I like how you are all singing and dancing during the chorus!''

Handling Possible Problems:

Some of the children may do the same movements for each animal.

Reinforce the behavior of the children who are doing different movements for each animal and mention that you know the others can too. Ask a child (who is having difficulty) to choose an animal like which he/she wishes to move. Reinforce the positive behavior after he/she does the movement. Some children may need individual attention.

Some children may stand still during the chorus.

Gently encourage the children to dance and sing-along. Tell them they can move any way they want, or offer them a suggestion, such as, jumping.

The Purpose:

SHADOW DANCING gives children the opportunity to discover the joy of moving with their own shadow. They also learn to be a leader by creating a special way of moving for their friends to "shadow." Children learn to appreciate the similarities and differences among their peers while working together in a group. This type of activity strengthens children's self-confidence while inspiring them to be leaders.

Kids' Glossary

Leap = To jump with one leg leading from one place on the ground to another.

Spin = To twirl your body around and around.

Curl = To make a curved shape with your body.

Zigzag = A zigzag pattern has short sharp turns like this: ⌇⌇⌇ .

Switch Roles = When two people are doing an activity together and one person is leading, you *switch roles* when it is the other person's turn to lead.

Twirling = To spin your body around in a circular pattern.

Stomping = To pound your feet heavily on the ground.

Creeping = To crawl slowly on the ground with your hands and knees.

Galloping = This is a fast movement; horses do it! You move one foot forward and then you move your other foot to join your first foot. Then, you quickly move your first foot forward again. You can have one foot lead for a while and then you can lead with the other foot.

Shadow Dancing #1:

Form a large circle with your friends. One of you begins by doing a special movement in the middle of a circle. Everyone in the circle moves their body just like you. When you are ready to stop, choose a friend to come into the center of the circle, and you go stand in his/her place. Continue until each of you has had a chance to lead a special movement for your friends to shadow.

Stationary Movement Ideas: Jumping, kicking, hopping, twisting, twirling, swaying, stomping, wiggling, stretching, bending, shaking, swinging, rising, dropping, leaning. Try these movements slow and fast, high and low, and strong and light.

Music: This activity can be done to any part of the music.

Shadow Dancing #2:

Everyone stands in a line, and the person in front begins by moving any way he/she would like around the room. The rest of you "shadow" the movements of the leader. Move in different patterns such as: sideways, backwards, zigzags and swirls. Continue with this activity until each of you has had a chance to lead a movement.

Movement Ideas: Skipping, running, walking, creeping, crawling, leaping, hopping, rolling, sliding, galloping and marching.
Try these movements: slow and fast, high and low, and strong and light.

Music: This activity can be done to any part of the music.

Advanced Shadow Dance: This activity is good for children over six years of age. In a circle of seven to ten people, one of you begins by creating a special movement for everyone else to shadow. Then, the person standing next to you creates a movement for everyone to shadow. All of you perform the first and then second movements together. Then, the third person comes up with a movement for everyone to shadow. All of you perform the first, second and then the third movements together. Continue until each of you has had a turn creating a movement, and you can perform each one smoothly in succession.

Shadow Dancing Activities

Note To Leader: *Do these next two activities outside with the sun casting shadows or set up a big floor lamp inside (away from the activity).*

Me And My Shadow:

Stand where you can easily see your shadow and begin by moving your body in place. Move high and low and from side to side. Make your body big and little. Move your hands, shoulders, arms, hips, legs, knees and feet. Jump, spin, wiggle, curl and stretch. Explore many different ways of moving with your shadow while standing in place.

Shadow Moves:

Find a place where you can easily see your shadow. Begin by moving all around the area. As you move, watch your shadow and try moving in all sorts of ways. For example: Leap, run, wiggle, hop, skip and crawl.

Shadow Dancing *Activities*

Note To Leader: *These next two activities are also called ''mirroring'' activities.*

Shadow One Part of Me:

Stand face to face with a friend. One of you begins by slowly moving your hands. Your friend moves his/her hands the same as you. As your hands move up, your friend's hands move up. Practice moving your hands in different directions. Move them up, down, in circles, zigzags, any pattern of which you can think. Then, let your partner have a turn leading as you follow the movement of his/her hands. Now, one of you start moving just your arms. Take turns leading until you have moved each part of your body as your partner ''shadows'' you.

Shadow All Of Me:

Standing face to face with your friend, begin by slowly moving your head. Your friend is watching you carefully, moving his/her head the same way as you. After a few seconds, slowly move your arms, then your hips, then your legs. Make sure your friend is following all of your movements as you begin to move your whole body any way you'd like. Move your nose, cheeks, mouth, eyes, elbows, shoulders, stomach, hips, legs and feet. Move up and down and from side to side. Move every part of your body slowly as your friend follows you. Then, switch roles and you shadow all of the movements of your friend.

Shadow Dancing

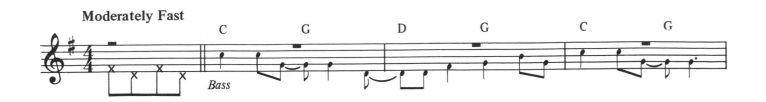

We're gon-na play a game called "Shad-ow Danc-in'."
2nd time: *Instrumental*

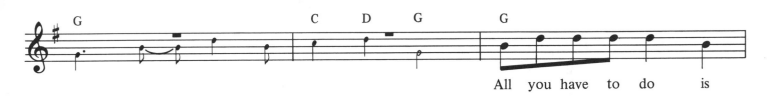

All you have to do is

fol-low me. Just

watch me close-ly and be my shad-ow.

Can you move your bod-y just like me?

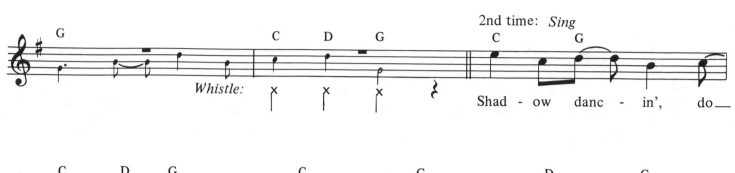

2nd time: *Sing*

Whistle:

Shad - ow danc - in', do___

___ what you see. *A* - Shad - ow danc - in' ex - act - ly.

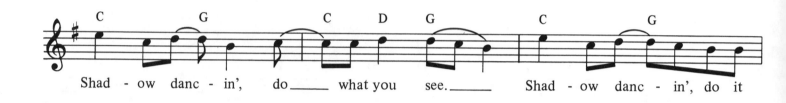

Shad - ow danc - in', do___ what you see.___ Shad - ow danc - in', do it

just like me.

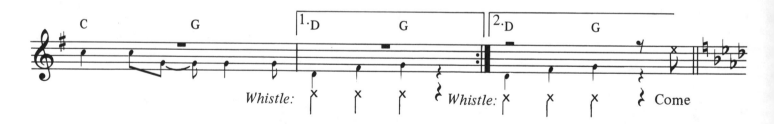

Whistle: *Whistle:* Come

on! Play a game called "Shad - ow Danc - in'."

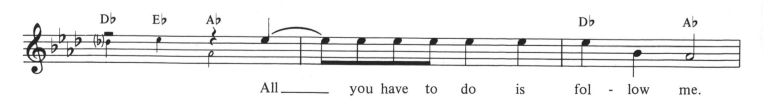

All___ you have to do is fol - low me.

Well, you're to watch me close - ly and

be my shad - ow. Can you

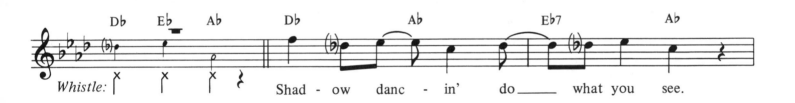

move your bod - y just____ like me?

Whistle: Shad - ow danc - in' do____ what you see.

Shad - ow danc - in' ex - act - ly. Shad - ow danc - in' do____

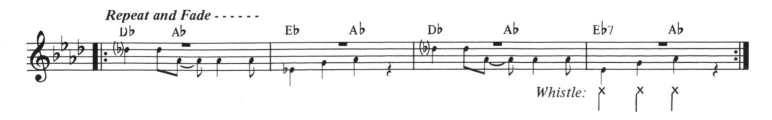

____ what you see. Shad - ow danc - in' do it just like me.

Repeat and Fade - - - - - -

Whistle:

Shadow Dancing *Lesson Plan*

Focus: *To give children the opportunity to create a special movement for their friends to "shadow."*

Objectives:

- To build self-confidence and feel comfortable initiating a movement.
- To learn how to work together as a group.
- To develop creativity and imagination.
- To increase strength, endurance and body coordination.
- To learn the difference between following and leading.
- To appreciate individual differences.

Procedure:

1) Form a large circle with the children.
2) Turn to the beginning of the chapter and do *Shadow Dancing #1* with the children.
3) Play the music for SHADOW DANCING after everyone has practiced their own special movements and remind the children to change leaders when they hear the whistle blow.
4) For an alternative, turn to *Shadow Dancing #2*. Practice the movements and then play the music for *SHADOW DANCING* again.

Reinforcing Positive Behavior:

When each child creates a different movement for everyone to shadow.

"Look how everyone is doing a different special movement!"

When the children are concentrating and following the movements of the leader.

"You are watching and following the leader so well!"

Handling Possible Problems:

A leader may choose a movement that is not safe.

It is very important to conduct movement sessions on a soft surface, like carpet or grass. However, if you are not moving on carpet, before you begin, tell the children which movements are not acceptable. Also, explain that it is because the floor is too hard and these types of movements should be done on soft carpet or grass. Here are movements that should **not** be allowed on a hard surface: Somersaults, cartwheels, handstands and headstands.

Some children may feel that the leader's movement is too difficult.

Tell the children to do the movement the best they can.

A leader may choose a movement that is truly too difficult for some of the other children.

Tell the leader that his/her movement is special but too hard for the other children. Ask him/her to choose another movement.

Some of the children may choose the same movements as someone else's special movement.

Tell each child who repeats a movement that it is still a good movement. Ask if they would like to try another movement now. Encourage them (without demanding) to think of another movement. **Note:** Very young children like to repeat the same movements. Do not force them to move differently if they don't wish to do so. Eventually, this will change, and all of the children will choose different movements.

Tummy Tango *Shapes and Movements of Food*

The Purpose:

TUMMY TANGO is all about food! Children develop creativity and imagination as they make shapes and move like their favorite and not-so-favorite food! This activity introduces healthy food to children and teaches the importance of good eating habits.

Kids' Glossary

Left = Everything to the side of your body in which your heart is located.

Right = Everything to the side of your body that is away from your heart.

Tango = A Latin-American dance.

Pomegranate = A red fruit about the size of an orange. It is thick-skinned and has many little reddish seeds inside.

Avocado = A mushy green fruit that is shaped like a pear.

Coconut = A round, brown-colored fruit with a hard, rough and fuzzy outer layer. The white inside is the part you can eat.

Plaintain = A type of a banana. Its outer layer is hard and green.

Gooseberry = A tiny little green berry.

Persimmon = An orange-colored round fruit that is soft inside when it's ripe.

Mango = An oval-shaped yellowish-red fruit from hot countries that has a sweet smell and taste. It has a firm outer skin and hard pit.

Chilipepper = A *HOT* little green pepper that has a tiny banana-like shape.

Piroshki = A little rectangular shaped Russian food. It has a crisp flaky outer layer made from dough and is usually filled with meat.

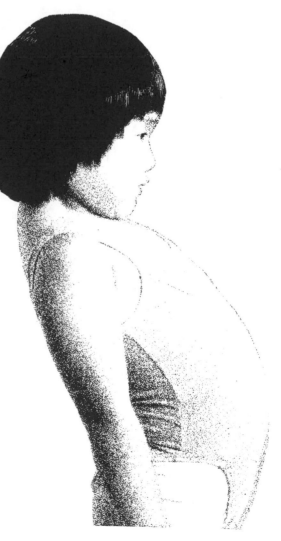

Tummy Tango *Activities*

"Banana"   "Watermelon"

Note To Leader: To enhance the following activities you may show real food or pictures of the food mentioned and discuss which ones have high nutritional value.

Food Shapes:

Spread out and make sure each of you has plenty of room to move freely. Begin by thinking about the different shapes of food. One of you at a time call out a food and everybody make your bodies into the shape of that food. *For example:* Make your body in the shape of a banana. Now try a big watermelon. Continue until each of you has had a turn suggesting a food. Notice how everyone makes their food shapes differently.

Here are some other healthy food ideas:
Fruits and vegetables: apple, orange, strawberry, grape, pineapple, pear, grape, cantaloupe, prune, potato, carrot, corn, lettuce, tomato, broccoli, cucumber, celery, mushroom and cauliflower.

Breads and Cereals: bread, muffin, cereals, rice, macaroni, noodle and pretzel.

Meat, fish, chicken, eggs and milk products: hamburger, lamb chop, hotdog, tuna fish, chicken leg, egg and swiss cheese.

Here are some different and unusal food ideas:
Donut, pizza, pickle, lollypop, pomegranate, avocado, coconut, plantain, gooseberry, persimmon, mango, chilipepper, piroshki and pudding.

Music: Section A

"Spaghetti Movement"

Food Moves:

Think about food that has interesting movements. One of you at a time call out a food for everyone to move like. For example: try moving like wiggly spaghetti. Continue until you have moved like many kinds of food.

Here are some other ideas:
Popping popcorn, melting popsicle, jiggly Jello, wiggly spaghetti, sticky peanut butter, rising bread, dripping water, pouring milk and a floppy hotdog.

Music: Section B

Let's Make a Meal:

Think about your favorite meal. One of you at a time describe your favorite meal to the rest of the group. Move like each food separately until the entire meal is complete.

Here are some ideas:
Peanut butter and jelly sandwich, banana and milk. Spaghetti and meatballs, salad and rolls. Orange, bowl of cereal and toast. Scrambled eggs, milk and muffin. Hamburger sandwich with lettuce, pickles, catsup, mustard and tomato.

The Tummy Tango:

Place your hands on your waist as you move your body to the left for a few seconds and sing:

"Tango To The Left, Tummy Tango."
(Try to move your tummy and hips too!)

Then sing:
"Tango To The Right, Tummy Tango"
(Move your body to the right.)

After a few seconds, sing:
"Tango To The Front, Tummy Tango"
(Move your body forward.)

Music: Section C

Then sing:
"Tango To The Back, Tummy Tango"
(Move your body backward.)

Now sing:
"Tango Way Down Low"
(Move your body to a squatting position.)

Then sing:
"Tango 'Till You Touch The Sky"
(Raise your body to a standing position and raise your arms up.)

Try to wiggle your tummy and hips throughout *THE TUMMY TANGO!*

Tummy Tango

C G
"Tan-go to the left." *All:* *Tum-my Tan-go!* "Tan-go to the right." *Tum-my Tan-go!*

Em Gmaj7/A
"Tan-go to the front" *Tum-my Tan-go!* Tan - go to the back. Tan -

to Coda ⊕ *D.S.* 𝄋 *al Coda*
go way down low. Tan - go 'til you touch the sky.

⊕ *CODA*
N.C. A Dm
Think a - bout your fav - 'rite food. What's the shape of an

A7 A7
egg? Think a - bout your fav - 'rite food. What's the shape of a

Dm D7
mush - room? Think a - bout your fav - 'rite food.

Gm7 Gm7/Bb Bbm7 Db6
What's the shape of a lol - li - pop?

F/C G/B Bb
Think a - bout your fav - 'rite food. What's the shape of a pick - le?

A7 N.C.
Let's all do the tum - my tan - go!

Tummy Tango Lesson Plan

Focus: *Making shapes and moving like different foods.*

Objectives:

- To develop creativity and imagination.
- To learn right and left.
- To expand understanding of spatial concepts (low and high, front and back.)
- To increase listening skills.
- To create different ways of moving like food and making the shapes of food.

Procedure:

1) Have the children spread out so that everyone has enough room to move.
2) Turn to the beginning of the chapter and do *Food Shapes* and *Food Moves*.
3) Turn to the *TUMMY TANGO* and have all of the children *face* you. When you practice "Tango to the left" you (the leader) move to the right as the children move to the left. Hold out your right arm as you move. This way the children will know which way to go and you can see them as they move in each direction. For "Tango to the right," hold out your left arm and move to your left as the children facing you move to their right. Continue until you feel the children have a basic understanding of the different directions.
4) Play the *TUMMY TANGO* as you and the children dance and sing-along. Remember to have the children face you during the chorus.

Reinforcing Positive Behavior:

When the children are making many different kinds of banana shapes.
"Look at all the different kinds of banana shapes you're making!"

When the children are doing the *TUMMY TANGO* well.
"You are really learning how to do the *TUMMY TANGO* in different directions. That's terrific!"

When the children are listening attentively.
"I can tell that you are all listening by the way you are moving!"

Handling Possible Problems:

Some of the children may feel frustrated learning right and left.
Reassure them that it gets easier with practice.

Friends *Quiet Time*

The Purpose:

Physical activity plays an essential part in the development of a child's health and happiness. However, after exercising, it is very important to rest and drink some water. *FRIENDS* provides children with a quiet and relaxing time to think and talk about the specialness of being and having a friend. Through reflection, discussion and song, children learn about the magic that exists in a friendship.

Friends *Activities*

Sit comfortably on the floor after drinking some water, listen to the song and discuss the following questions with the group. After hearing the first question, one of you at a time answer, and then go on to the next question.

Reflection and Discussion:

Close your eyes for a moment and think about one of your special friends.

- What do you like best about your friend?
- How do you show your friend that you like him/her?
- What do you like to do with your special friend?
- What would you do if your friend felt sad?
- Is there anything else you would like to share about your special friend?

Friends

From "Rose Petal Place," A David Kirschner Production

Show Me What You Feel *Creative Expression of Feelings*

The Purpose:

SHOW ME WHAT YOU FEEL provides children with a creative and constructive outlet for their feelings. This type of activity helps children identify and express what they feel and teaches them that it is healthy to do so. In addition, children develop sensitivity and compassion toward others.

Kids' Glossary

Proud = You feel proud when you have done something well and it makes you feel good about yourself!

Jealous = A person may feel jealous of someone else when he/she feels that this person has something that he/she wants.

Confused = To feel uncertain or not sure about something.

Excited = To have a strong feeling about something.

Acting Out = To show a feeling through your movements so that other people will know how you feel.

Several Seconds = Approximately 5 to 7 seconds.

Show Me What You Feel Activities

My Face Shows Feelings:

Begin by discussing the many different feelings we all are capable of feeling. Feelings like: happy, sad, mad, shy, proud, bored, jealous, funny, scared, silly, tired, hungry, surprized, confused, excited and love. Then, choose one feeling at a time and everyone together shows that feeling on their face. For example: Can you show the group a *happy* face? How about a *sad* face? Continue until you have shown as many feelings as possible.

My Body Shows Feelings:

Begin by making sure that each of you has enough room to stand without bumping into anyone or anything. One of you calls out a feeling for each person in the group to make into a body shape. For example, *shy*. Can you make your body in a shape that shows you are feeling *shy*? How about *angry*? Continue until you have made the body shapes of as many feelings as possible.

Feelings Make Me Move:

Now you can move like the different feelings for which you made faces and body shapes. Call out one feeling at a time and move your body in a way that shows that feeling. For example, how do you move when you feel *happy*? How do you move when you feel shy, mad, tired, sad, excited, strong, afraid, surprized, hungry, silly and love. Continue until you have shown many different feelings though movement.

Music: Section A

Show Me What You Feel *Activities*

I Feel Like. . . !:

In this activity you'll be able to show each other how you move when you feel like doing different activities. For example, dancing. How do you move when you feel like dancing? Play *SHOW ME WHAT YOU FEEL* or another favorite song to which everyone can do their favorite dancing. Move each part of your body as you dance all around the room. Now, one of you think about another activity you enjoy. How about skating? Everyone move like you are skating. Continue until each of you has had a turn suggesting an idea.

Here are some other activities:
Running, playing baseball, soccer, volleyball, handball, basketball, tennis, riding a bike, skiing or swimming.

Music: Section B

Can You Guess What I'm Feeling?:

One of you at a time enters the center of the circle and acts out a feeling. After several seconds, choose a friend in the circle to guess what you are feeling. When your friend answers correctly, change places and then he/she chooses a feeling to which to move. Continue until each of you has had a turn acting out as many feelings as possible.

Show Me What You Feel *Lesson Plan*

Focus: *To learn how to identify and express feelings.*

Objectives:

- To understand different feelings.
- To physically express feelings.
- To strengthen sensitivity towards others.
- To develop imagination.
- To build endurance and mind/body coordination.

Procedure:

1) Have the children spread out so that everyone has enough room to move.
2) Turn to *Feelings Make Me Move* and do the activity with the children.
3) Turn to *I Feel Like...* and do that activity with the children.
4) Play the music for *SHOW ME WHAT YOU FEEL* as you and the children dance and sing-along.

Reinforcing Positive Behavior:

When the children are creating different movements to express one specific feeling.

"I can see from the way you are moving that you really understand the meaning of 'happy.' And you're all showing it in a different way!" Give examples if you wish.

When the children choose different ways of moving to show each feeling.

"Each feeling makes you move in a different way, right?" Give examples.

When the children are listening to the lyric.

"You are all listening so carefully!"

Handling Possible Problems:

Some of the children may do the same movements to express different feelings.

Reinforce the behavior of those children who are moving in different ways to show different feelings. Mention that you know the others can too. Practice moving to different feelings without music again. Ask these children to choose a feeling to which they would like to move. Perhaps they choose, "mad." Communicate that you can tell by the way they are stomping their feet that they know how to show that feeling! Ask them to pick another feeling.

Some of the children may not feel comfortable doing this activity and expressing their feelings.

Allow these children to watch and join in when they are ready. Do not force them to participate.

Autoharp Transpositions

AUTOHARP HINTS: There will be chords in this book that do not exist on the autoharp; try these solutions for substitutions:

1) For major, minor or 7th chords:
   a. Drop the 7th and try just the plain chord.
   b. For a minor chord, try its relative major chord (a third higher).
   c. Chords with 6ths, major 7ths, 6/9, major 9ths, just use the major chord.
   d. Chords with minor 6ths, minor 7ths, etc. use the minor chord.
   e. Chords with 7–5, 7+5, 7–9, 9ths, 11ths and 13ths, use the 7th chord.

2) For augmented and diminished chords, replace them with 7th chords, BUT try each one carefully, and listen to the sound.

Here's an easy transposition chart called the "Circle of Fifths," which should help you by enabling you to count the number of notes you wish to transpose by half-steps.

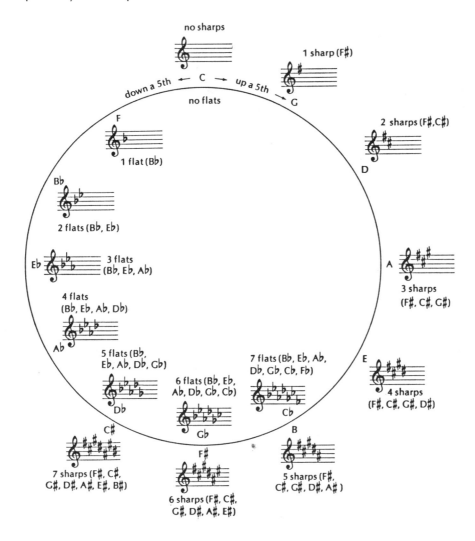

The following pairs of keys are enharmonic equivalents: Db and C#, Gb and F#, Cb and B. They sound the same but are spelled differently.

Guitar Chords

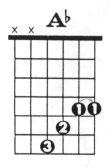

A♭

A♭m

A

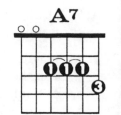

Am

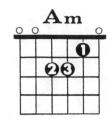

A7

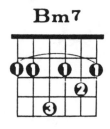

A♯/B♭

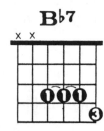

B♭7

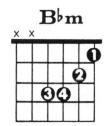

B♭m

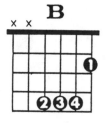

B

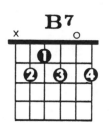

B7

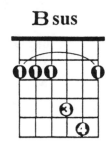

Bm7

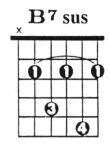

B sus

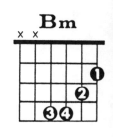

B7 sus

Bm

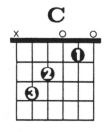

C

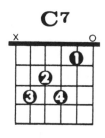

C7

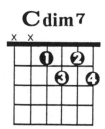

Cdim7

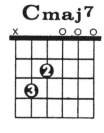

Cmaj7

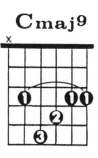

Cmaj9

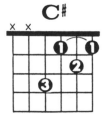

C♯

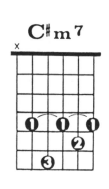

C♯m7

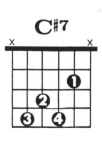

C♯7

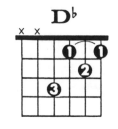

D♭

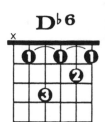

D♭6

D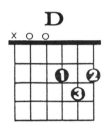
Dm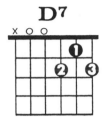
D⁷
Dm⁷
Dm⁹

D♯dim⁷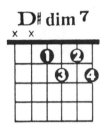
E♭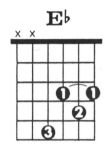
E♭⁷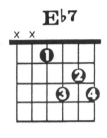

E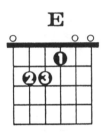
Em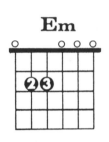
E⁷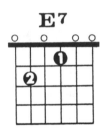
Em⁷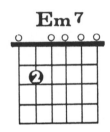

F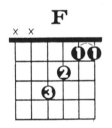
F⁷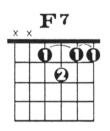
F♯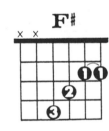
F♯m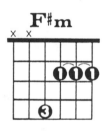

G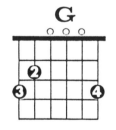
G⁷
Gsus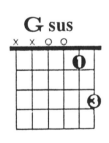
G⁶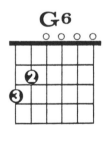
Gmaj⁷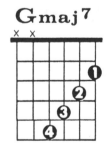
Gm⁷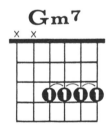

G♯

Piano Chords

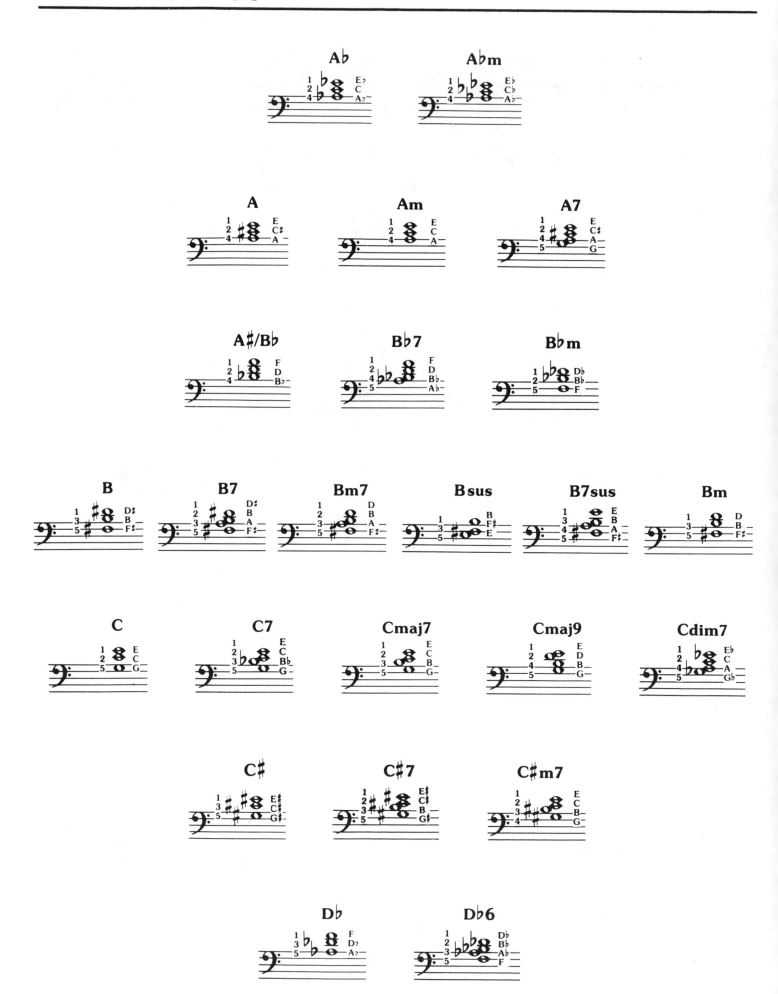

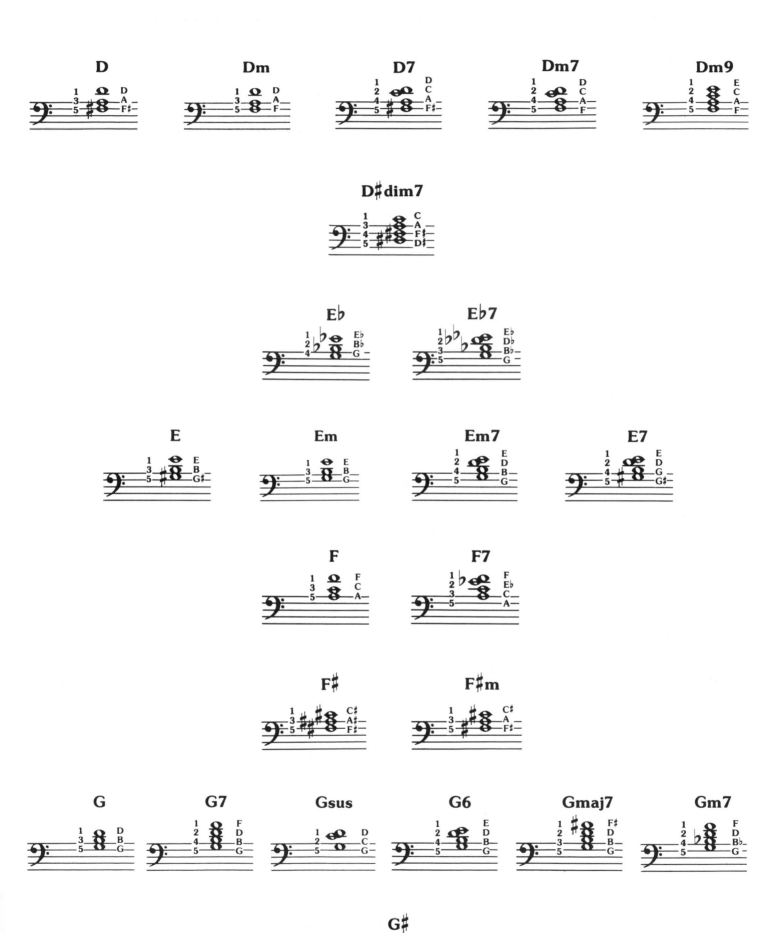

Selections from this book appear on the Good Housekeeping™ *Kids Sing Along Video*
KIDS IN MOTION Videos Volumes 1 and 2 — available at your local store.

All of the songs in this book are available on record,
cassette or CD through:

 YOUNGHEART RECORDS
Dept. HLP
10701 Holder Street
Cypress, CA 90630

Write for prices and the latest catalog.

CATALOG NO.	DESCRIPTION
YM001-R	WE ALL LIVE TOGETHER Volume 1 Record
YM001-CN	WE ALL LIVE TOGETHER Volume 1 Cassette
YM002-R	WE ALL LIVE TOGETHER Volume 2 Record
YM002-CN	WE ALL LIVE TOGETHER Volume 2 Cassette
YM002-CD	WE ALL LIVE TOGETHER Volume 2 CD
YM003-R	WE ALL LIVE TOGETHER Volume 3 Record
YM003-CN	WE ALL LIVE TOGETHER Volume 3 Cassette
YM004-R	WE ALL LIVE TOGETHER Volume 4 Record
YM004-CN	WE ALL LIVE TOGETHER Volume 4 Cassette
YM005-R	ON THE MOVE WITH GREG & STEVE Record
YM005-CN	ON THE MOVE WITH GREG & STEVE Cassette
YM005-CD	ON THE MOVE WITH GREG & STEVE CD
YM006-R	QUIET MOMENTS WITH GREG & STEVE Record
YM006-CN	QUIET MOMENTS WITH GREG & STEVE Cassette
YM006-CD	QUIET MOMENTS WITH GREG & STEVE CD
YM007-R	KIDDING AROUND WITH GREG & STEVE Record
YM007-CN	KIDDING AROUND WITH GREG & STEVE Cassette
YM007-CD	KIDDING AROUND WITH GREG & STEVE CD
YM008-R	KIDS IN MOTION Record
YM008-CN	KIDS IN MOTION Cassette
YM008-CD	KIDS IN MOTION CD
YM009-R	HOLIDAYS AND SPECIAL TIMES Record
YM009-CN	HOLIDAYS AND SPECIAL TIMES Cassette
YM009-CD	HOLIDAYS AND SPECIAL TIMES CD
YM012-R	GREG & STEVE PLAYING FAVORITES Record
YM012-CN	GREG & STEVE PLAYING FAVORITES Cassette
YM012-CD	GREG & STEVE PLAYING FAVORITES CD
YM011-V	GREG & STEVE LIVE IN CONCERT Video
YM012-V	GREG & STEVE MUSICAL ADVENTURES Video

Also published by Hal Leonard Publishing Corp. and available at your local store...
00815003	WE ALL LIVE TOGETHER Plus Song & Activity Book and Leader's Guide
00815028	GREG & STEVE THE WORLD IS A RAINBOW Songs for Kids

MusicTivity™ **Book & Audio Collections**
00330609	LOVE IS... Book/Cassette
00330608	LOVE IS... Book/CD
00330607	EVERYBODY HAS MUSIC INSIDE Book/Cassette
00330606	EVERYBODY HAS MUSIC INSIDE Book/CD